6 STEPS To a Schooled Horse

RELAXATION • RHYTHM • CONTACT
STRAIGHTNESS • IMPULSION • COLLECTION

SUSAN MCBANE

David and Charles

A DAVID & CHARLES BOOK
Copyright © David & Charles Limited 2009

David & Charles is an F+W Media Inc. company
4700 East Galbraith Road
Cincinnati, OH 45236

First published in the UK and USA in 2009

Text copyright © Susan McBane 2009
Photographs copyright © Horsepix, 2009, except those on pages 4, 6, 7, 8, 10, 12, 13, 16, 17, 20
(top), 23(top), 24, 28, 29 (lower left and lower right), 33 (lower), 34 (right), 35, 36, 37, 38, 39,
40, 41, 42, 44, 48, 52, 53 (top), 54, 66, 67, 72, 73, 76, 77, 78, 82, 83, 84, 85 (lower left, centre and
right), 86, 87 (left), 88, 90, 91, 97, 99, 100, 101, 104, 105, 107, 108, 111, 113 (top left and right),
117, 118, 120, 132, 134 and 142.
Illustrations copyright © David & Charles, 2009

Susan McBane has asserted her right to be identified as author of this work in accordance
with the Copyright, Designs and Patents Act, 1988.

A catalogue record for this book is available from the British Library.

ISBN-13: 978-0-7153-2991-7 hardback
ISBN-10: 0-7153-2991-X hardback

Printed in Singapore by KHL
for David & Charles
Brunel House   Newton Abbot   Devon

Commissioning Editor: Jane Trollope
Desk Editor: Emily Rae
Art Editor: Martin Smith
Senior Designer: Jodie Lystor
Production Controller: Beverley Richardson
Photography: Horsepix. With its roots in horse country and staffed by horse people,
Horsepix is a leading provider of high quality equestrian photography.

Visit our website at www.davidandcharles.co.uk

David & Charles books are available from all good bookshops; alternatively you can contact
our Orderline on 0870 9908222 or write to us at FREEPOST EX2 110, D&C Direct, Newton
Abbot, TQ12 4ZZ (no stamp required UK only); US customers call 800-289-0963 and
Canadian customers call 800-840-5220.

CONTENTS

Preparation

They say wars are won on the training ground and competitions are won at home. Preparation is everything, and your groundwork, homework and initial familiarization are an essential basis for progress and success.

WHAT ARE THE 'SCALES OF TRAINING'?

The purpose of this book is to explain what the Scales of Training are to riders who may not know much about them; sometimes they are also called the Training Ladder.

The Scales of Training are stages in a systematic programme of psychological and gymnastic development of the basic qualities required of good riding horses, whatever work they are intended for. The scales were refined in Germany over the 19th and 20th centuries and are now used internationally, but the qualities that they deal with were recognized and used in schooling centuries earlier by the European classical masters.

As a system of schooling and development, the scales have proved invaluable to generations of riders who have simply wanted to produce a good riding horse, for whatever reason. Every horse needs thorough basic training to enable him to progress with as few problems as possible, and the training scales give him that – through his trainer, of course.

Another advantage of the scales is that, although they are laid out in a particular order (see opposite page) they are flexible and can accommodate the needs of different individuals. Also, it is not simply a case of teaching a horse one particular scale or quality and then 'promoting' him to the next. All working horses, throughout their lives, need to revisit all the earlier scales – indeed the most advanced horse may be given regular refresher lessons that take him through each scale in one schooling session, as his trainer revises his mastery of each scale.

The beauty of the system is that it provides a clear, time-proven 'road map' of goals or destinations. You do not have to achieve perfection in one scale before progressing to the next, but the horse must be pretty competent and reliable in each before moving on.

When something goes wrong in schooling it can often be traced back to a previous stage not having been adequately absorbed, or to the schooling and progression having been rushed – a very common mistake. If this occurs, step back down the ladder to find out where the problem originates and give that rung, or scale, more attention.

Many riders call themselves 'just happy hackers' but to be safe out hacking you need to be a good rider with a controllable horse. The Training Scales are important and valuable for every horse and rider.

Each of the scales concentrates on an individual quality, but they are all interdependent. For instance, you cannot obtain a confident, regular rhythm if the horse is not relaxed, and you cannot expect collection from a horse who is not straight and capable of impulsion.

The six qualities shown are sub-divided into three *overlapping* phases of development. The first three belong in the first phase, which is Familiarization (preliminary ridden training), the middle four are encompassed in the second phase, which is Pushing Power (development of forward thrust) and the last three make up the development of Carrying Capacity, when the horse carries his and his rider's weight more on to his hindquarters and legs, a little further back than his natural centre of gravity.

When a horse is capable of the full programme, he is said to have 'throughness'. The aids and their effects pass freely through his body from hindquarters to mouth and vice versa because he is strong, supple (or 'loose') and mentally attuned to his rider, who also must be attuned to the horse.

Every riding horse can benefit from this physical and psychological education programme, even if he never reaches the end of it. It results in a well-behaved horse who is a pleasure to ride, and whose health and working life are extended through the creation of calmness, cooperation and the correct development of his natural physique and capabilities.

The scales are relevant whatever standard you are at. With more advanced horses such, as this lovely mare performing trot half-pass, the scales act as a revision tool or a troubleshooting method if problems occur, when you can go back down the ladder to find out their roots.

This applies just as much to experienced, older horses who have not been schooled or developed correctly and are showing various behavioural and physical problems.

The scales are usually set out as, from the beginning, Rhythm, Relaxation, Contact, Impulsion, Straightness and Collection. Some experts and masters of equitation prefer a change in their order, with which the I agree, so that they run **Relaxation, Rhythm, Contact, Straightness, Impulsion** and **Collection**. The reasons for these two changes are as follows:

1. without Relaxation – a calm mind and tension-free body – nothing can be achieved because a horse's mind (the easily-alarmed mind of a prey animal) cannot learn if he is not calm, and his body cannot develop correctly and beneficially if he is stiff or tense
2. it is more logical to aim for a good degree of Straightness before Impulsion because the last thing that you want is a crooked horse thrusting along and further developing the muscles that are creating his crooked way of going.

QUALITIES OF THE SCALES

We often see, in any form of riding, horses performing in a travesty of what they would be capable of if trained properly, with knowledge, competence and empathy. It is damaging to push a horse through the scales so as to make him perform certain movements and appear schooled when he is not, and it produces an ugly, uncomfortable result.

Correct and fair schooling involves *giving the horse time* to understand what we are asking, to develop physically and mentally, and become fairly competent in one scale before moving on to another. He needs to accomplish *quality* in his work and to perform it with relative ease before he can benefit from it and progress, not to be pushed and pulled around, held up and in and kicked here and there. In truly good riding, lightness and cooperation are our goals.

In each scale there are different things that you should be looking out for.

Relaxation

If the horse's mind is not calm his body will also be tense, and his attention will not be on his work but on his survival. He is a prey animal whose prime instinct is staying alive. In this condition, no horse can learn properly or work well. He needs to be confident in and trusting of his rider not to cause him pain, discomfort or anxiety, so that he *can* relax. His body will swing comfortably and feel loose, and his face will look contented and interested in his work.

Walking on a long rein is useful for so many things. It prepares the horse for work during his warm-up by limbering him up; it helps to relax and calm a horse; it provides a mental rest during a schooling session and helps the horse to wind down after work. It also really helps to teach a horse to walk out, and that he can walk out with no restriction from the rider, and it confirms to the rider the horse's natural rhythm

Rhythm

Every horse has a natural rhythm to each gait. When he is carrying the weight of a rider his balance is disturbed and thus so is his natural rhythm. This scale enables the horse to find his rhythm under weight. He needs a well-balanced rider with a reasonable sense of rhythm herself, who has found, and allowed the horse to find, his natural rhythm. He must work with a regular beat so that his strides are of equal duration and cover equal distances. His rhythm must remain consistent on straight lines, curves and transitions and during all movements.

The Relaxation scale encompasses looseness or suppleness. Thorney, an older, former event horse, now a hunter, keeps up his suppleness with lateral work (this is leg yield).

The long rein principle can be applied to all gaits during preparation and warming up or to gradually cool down after fast work.

Contact

Your contact must *not*, in any way, cause your horse discomfort, pain, confusion, alarm or fear. A steady, flexible contact, of the strength with which you would hold a small bird in your hand without hurting it, is a good starting point until the horse becomes well-balanced enough to achieve the ultimate self-carriage on the weight of the rein – which is still a contact. Humane, modern riding requires that the horse does *not* lean on the bit for 'support' or require 'holding up', but finds self-balance from an early stage, using the bit as a genuine communication/information point. The only things that put a healthy, sound horse out of balance are an unbalanced rider or being asked to perform too-difficult movements, and too soon.

Straightness

Most horses are naturally crooked. Straightness demands that on straight lines and curves the horse's hind feet follow the same track or plane as his forefeet and that his spine and body follow the straight or curved track that he is following. When straightness is achieved, the energetic forces stimulated by the rider pass evenly through the body and produce the horse's best movement with the minimum of effort.

The basic, correct position for your hands is on a straight line from your elbow through your hand to your horse's mouth. This gives you the most direct feel on your horse's mouth and is your 'headquarters' position, to which you should always return your hands if you need to move them from it.

Impulsion

Impulsion is a springy, thrusting power, not speed, which surges up from the hindquarters to the mouth and is tactfully controlled by the rider to produce 'contained energy' and brilliant gaits. Muscles work harder to create the lift and power: impulsion cannot be produced by weak, unfit or green horses. Sustained impulsion is schooled for by the rider, the horse's natural paces being enhanced by suppleness (looseness), thrust and the beginnings of cadence.

Collection

This is a state in which the horse can produce lift in the forehand with lowered hindquarters. He is in perfect balance and self-control (self-carriage), with strong hindquarters producing forward, upward energy. His weight being borne further back lightens the forehand, saving his forelegs and giving the rider the same exhilarating feel and featherlight control experienced in a speedboat or a powerful sports car.

Do not think that all this is beyond you. Although not every horse has the conformation or potential physical and mental strength to achieve collection, many more could get much further than they do with systematic, patient and competent training. This book will help you with that.

Emma canters Thorney easily down a narrow corridor of poles (having first walked and trotted down it). This exercise familiarizes horse and rider with the feel of straightness, or reminds them of it, and so helps them to achieve and maintain it more easily.

THE TRAINING LADDER

The Training Scales are often described as a pyramid or, quite commonly, as the Training Ladder. The bottom rung, essential to all the others, is Relaxation; the second is Rhythm which is not possible without Relaxation and which leads to confident, balanced gaits, making the third rung, Contact, easier to achieve. Straightness comes fourth, then you can correctly develop the fifth rung which is Impulsion. The sixth rung, the top of the ladder, is Collection.

   The six scales are interdependent and further divided as shown. The first three are involved in Familiarization with basic schooling, the middle four with the development of Pushing Power from the hindquarters and legs, and the final three comprise Carrying Capacity, in which the horse is able to adjust his weight back and, due to strengthened hindquarters and legs from correct schooling, carry his body - under the weight of a rider and saddle - with a much higher degree of ease and safety than if he were developed incorrectly or not at all.

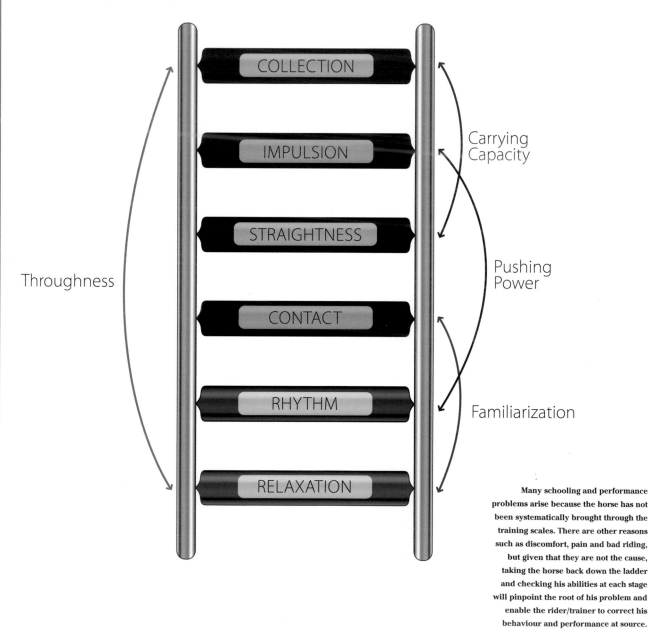

Many schooling and performance problems arise because the horse has not been systematically brought through the training scales. There are other reasons such as discomfort, pain and bad riding, but given that they are not the cause, taking the horse back down the ladder and checking his abilities at each stage will pinpoint the root of his problem and enable the rider/trainer to correct his behaviour and performance at source.

BEFORE YOU BEGIN

At this point, I should stress that this book deals with schooling a horse under saddle, regardless of his age or whether or not he is a blank canvas, has had good previous handling and riding or has been spoiled in some way. The important subjects of bringing up foals and youngstock and of backing and riding away young horses are covered in many excellent books, videos and DVDs.

This book picks up where they leave off. It assumes that the horse is fully used to his tack, accepts a comfortable bit in his mouth, a saddle and a competent, lightweight rider on his back, understands basic vocal commands learnt from foalhood and during ground training, maybe on the lunge or, later, long-reins, and is riding away confidently, obediently and willingly.

The book is also relevant to older horses who have been spoiled, perhaps rushed through their training, deprived of a proper education or taught badly, and are now in new (your) hands. The scales are relevant to all.

Whatever you want a horse to do, if he is not comfortable he will concentrate as much on his discomfort as on his work. Checking tack for comfortable fit before work is important.

WHAT ARE YOU DEALING WITH?

The scales begin with Relaxation so you can actually have in mind and begin using the scales system from day one. Most genuine horsemen and horsewomen have a strong, quiet, still and innately kind aura about them and create a safe atmosphere that horses respond well to and thrive within, so the system can be used as a framework or concept in the handling of foals and young horses, even years before they are ready to work on the lunge or long-reins.

A young horse who has been brought up on the stud in this kind of atmosphere and who has been fairly disciplined, as in a herd, taught basic vocal commands, been well-handled and taught to behave well when led, walking freely straight forward without anyone hanging on to his head, has already learnt relaxation and a degree of rhythm when under human control. Most horses do not have a problem with rhythm when they are at liberty and are *not* wearing ill-fitting, restrictive rugs. These can certainly affect a horse's action badly, even when he is not wearing them.

If you are fortunate enough to acquire a well-handled young horse, your work will be much easier. If you acquire

The noseband, of whatever type, must be loose enough to allow a finger to be easily slid under it all round the horse's head, including over the bridge of the nose and under the jaw. Tight nosebands are a very common cause of discomfort in horses.

If youngsters are brought up and schooled with patience and allowed sufficient time they take to their lessons so much more easily and last longer in work. This recently backed youngster is being led around by the trainer, before being lunged with a rider, to get him used to the feel of carrying weight.

one who has had little handling, he may be far from relaxed and, because he cannot lead well in-hand, trying this will disrupt his own natural rhythm. Your job from day one of your life together is to adopt the demeanour described previously, to put him at ease from then on. For the sake of the future purity of his gaits, you also need to teach him as soon as possible to walk out freely and straight in-hand, working to the voice and using light aids on the headcollar to direct him. Maintain the atmosphere during backing and riding away.

Before you embark on this schooling programme, your horse needs a modicum of schooling – his ABC. A young horse or a green older one should be calmly and willingly obeying clear, well-timed physical and vocal aids; he should be starting and stopping obediently, turning both ways and unafraid of a schooling whip. He should be walking and trotting on confidently, but maybe not cantering, under saddle, and that is all. In other words, he is what is called backed and riding away.

If you take on an older, spoiled horse, again your demeanour is key to letting him know how things are done with you. Spoiled horses often calm down and stop being defensive, on the ground or under saddle, once they are with someone who behaves and thinks like a horseman, although some take time, and others are no job for a novice. You may need to make a complete assessment of his bodily condition – weight, health, conformation and soundness (although if he is new to you presumably you had him vetted before purchase).

With any new horse, it is always worth having an equine profile (comprehensive blood test) to check his general health and see if anything needs putting right or investigating further. His teeth and worming should be attended to no matter what his previous owner has told you, and his vaccination status checked. Check his feet and his back, and make sure that the tack you plan to use fits him really comfortably and is what will help him.

If he has health problems, take veterinary advice on how to manage him during his recovery. You can use this time before you start riding him to get to know him so that he picks up your ways, learns your voice commands and aids from the ground and gradually soaks up the calm, safe atmosphere of his new home and companions.

A three-year-old getting off to a good start. He is calm and relaxed and so is his trainer. The training aid he is wearing attaches to rings on his roller, passed through the bit (he is being lunged from the cavesson) and down through his forelegs back to the roller. It is loose and allows the horse to stretch his nose right down to the ground. Being made of leather, it is weighty enough to encourage the horse to carry his head and neck down without any kind of restriction whatsoever.

SPOILED HORSES

This sort of treatment alone should go a good way towards settling a horse down, but if he has any unwanted behaviour patterns under saddle, you, or someone else competent and not rough, may have to deal with them. To understand your horse's mind and the reasons behind his behaviour, you would do well to read *The Truth About Horses: a guide to understanding and training your horse* by Dr Andrew McLean, founder of the Australian Equine Behaviour Centre (see Further Reading, page 150). It is an inspiring and enlightening book to read, and the practices it teaches are all based on the scientific and practical knowledge we now have about how horses really learn and why they behave as they do.

'Bad behaviour' is usually the result of misunderstanding and confusion on the part of the horse, and is often due to poorly executed and timed instructions from the rider. Horses learn by the association of ideas, linking experiences with consequent behaviour. But this means they learn very fast (both 'right' and 'wrong' behaviour – to the horse it is all just 'appropriate') and they form firm habits quickly. However, because of the horse's mental functioning, it is possible to 'overshadow' bad memories and form good habits.

It may not be possible to extinguish very frightening experiences completely, but they should be considerably reduced if the rider applies and releases correct aids at the right moments, and never applies inappropriate aids. It is no good saying to a horse, 'Sorry, I didn't mean it.' Timing is crucial in horse training, bad timing being a major factor in creating unwanted behaviour. This is usually defensive, although we may not see it as such, and is often due to confusion.

The basic principles of the methods of equitation science, to use its formal name, are used throughout this book, as although it is primarily aimed at explaining the traditional scales it does not necessarily recommend the use of traditional methods.

As I ride and teach using classical methods (preferring old French/Portuguese principles), I use the techniques of that school of thought as well, in a way that fits in with equitation science. I feel that readers will find that these methods, far from being a confusing mixture, form a logical, simple and effective blend that horses respond to quickly and calmly.

Horses are brilliant at working out what we want, but that is no excuse for applying muddy aids or inconsistent techniques. A combination of the best of the old and the new proves very successful.

YOUR OWN SKILLS

In order to ride well you need certain basic skills and knowledge that will enable you to do the job properly.

A good rider must:

- be able to ride in good balance and with an independent seat and hands so that you never hang on your horse's mouth, restrict him by propping yourself on his neck when jumping, ride crookedly or grip with your legs except in an emergency. All such errors upset and confuse the horse and he may either become hyper or shut down
- have feel, coordination and muscular control of your body so that you can control your position and movements, sense what the horse is doing, and apply your aids and use your body at the right times so that he can relate them to himself and move 'appropriately'
- have a good sense of timing and the ability to concentrate on what you are doing so that you do the right thing at the right time, and don't 'miss the moment'. Timing is crucial in schooling horses; you need to concentrate and grasp when to give an aid and when to stop it, so that your horse learns the right response. Above all, forget the old idea that you need to 'do something at every stride'.

For more advice/guidance see the Further Reading section on page 150.

This is the commonest way of holding a single rein. In general, you should have a gentle but reassuring weight of contact appropriate to your horse.

Concentrating on holding your rein between your index finger and thumb enables you to open and close your lower fingers to give or take enough rein for most circumstances. You can open your lower fingers and give your horse 5cm (2in) or so of rein, as needed.

You can take the rein back again by simply closing your lower fingers again. In this way, you do not need to move your arm forward at all: again, this is a minimalist, classical aid, which does not move you at all from your base-line position.

Seat and legs

The rider's seat and legs are the main point of contact with the horse, and riding is better for both horse and rider if the rider can learn to ride mainly with them, and pay far less attention to the hands than is normally done. Apparently, Mestre Nuno Oliveira was always saying: 'Try to use a little less hand', which is excellent advice.

The rider's thighs are an often-overlooked part of the aiding equipment. They form part of the seat, and part of the legs and horses are sensitive to pressure from them. Most riders use far too much lower leg, and particularly heel. Try to be more subtle with your aids. Think first of using your seat and thighs to direct your horse, then your lower leg and your heel only if necessary.

The leg aids can gradually be reduced until the horse answers a nudge from the seat bones to move off or up to a different gait. The seat bones can also be used to guide the horse directionally – left seat bone forward or weighted means 'Please go left' and vice versa. A horse who lifts up into canter from conventional leg aids can become accustomed to responding to an upward lift and forward placement of the inside seat bone, returning to trot when the seat bone is brought back into line.

Halting or slowing simply with the seat and thighs is much more rewarding than pulling the horse to a halt with the reins. The rider simply stops moving their seat (and thighs) with the movements of the horse and keeps the hands still; most horses will slow or halt. If they don't, just saying whatever command they associate with it, such as 'Whoa' or 'Stand' almost always does the trick.

To ride well with the seat and legs, the rider needs to be able to keep the seat muscles loose and the hips opened out across the saddle, draping the legs down the horse's sides, in tone but not rigid or stiff, and certainly not pressing on to the ribcage all the time.

This is the leg position for most riding and the one that shows the classic straight line from the rider's ear, through the shoulder, the elbow and hip to the ankle or heel. Held at the ready but without pressure, it is the 'headquarters' position, guiding and controlling the hindquarters and hind legs. It is used as the outside leg for turns and circles, lateral work, canter aids and, both legs together brushed back to here, for rein back.

An on-the-girth position, or just behind it, is used as the inside leg to ask for 'bend' in turns and circles, in practice moving the ribcage away from it to give the impression of lateral spinal bend.

A leg position in front of the girth can be used as the outside leg to help move the forehand over away from it or to move an individual foreleg. Some riders use it to encourage foreleg extension once impulsion from behind has been achieved, such as in extended gaits in an advanced horse.

A more extreme behind-the-girth position and sometimes further back than here, this is used for advanced work and to ask for more elevation in the collected, advanced gaits such as piaffe, passage and High School airs.

WHY USE THE SCALES OF TRAINING?

The Scales of Training give you a reliable, guiding programme of where to start and where to go next. This book will give you the judgment and techniques to get as far as your horse can go. Correctly progressing through the scales and revising them where necessary lays the foundations for any kind of riding, including jumping. They are suitable for *any* riding horse in any discipline, including jumpers, who need a solid base of flatwork to make them supple, agile and strong enough to jump.

The scales are sometimes seen by those inexperienced in their use as levels of 'promotion': a horse moving 'up' to a 'higher' level until he reaches Collection. They are, but they are qualities that are needed at *all* levels of accomplishment. They have a dual purpose in that they are logically progressive, but their qualities are needed

constantly by any well- or fully-schooled horse. A horse presented as 'in Collection' is not truly there if he is not Relaxed, has an erratic Rhythm, is fussing with his bit (Contact) rather than gently playing with it, is crooked (Straightness) and does not have Impulsion.

The scales, then, are not just a checklist of success with a box by each one for you to tick before you move on, although you can do that. They need to be revisited constantly at all stages of schooling to keep the *quality* of your horse's work up to scratch. We see so many glaring examples of truly dreadful work being rewarded with prizes in competition (which unfortunately many people regard as the criterion for 'doing well') that it is clear that many riders and trainers do not use the scales properly, if at all, or they misinterpret them.

Make sure that your reins are long enough to allow a genuinely free-rein walk, like this. Shorter reins inhibit the horse psychologically and therefore physically, so he never experiences the completely free head that encourages relaxation and muscle health.

Bucking

As a guide to re-schooling, let's take bucking as an example. We know that bucking is triggered by over-feeding, under-exercising (including lack of freedom), exuberance, habitual behaviour, pain and discomfort in the back or an uncomfortable saddle and/or girth. It is also a sign that the horse is not 'forward' or, to use more scientific terminology, his 'go response' is not in place. For a horse to be 'forward' he must respond almost unconsciously and instantly to a rider's aids, in whatever direction they are indicating.

Forwardness is taught as part of the Rhythm scale, along with balance, which is an ongoing necessity. If a horse starts bucking, therefore, and you have eliminated all the other reasons for it, you can assume that he does not go 'forward' to the extent that he is always ready to answer his rider's aids. He may move but not crisply or energetically and not at once.

Go back to Rhythm and establish that you are still familiar with his natural rhythm. Once he is moving effortlessly within it, you can re-school forwardness more easily because the rhythm inspires the horse to go on to his next step: he will be glad to go forward unless he is naturally lazy.

After a break, take up a long rein (hardly any contact), and give a light aid to 'Walk on'. If he does not respond within a second, keep repeating the aid a little more strongly until he does, and add your vocal command, which he should habitually respond to from groundwork. Keep applying the aid, maybe reinforced behind your inside leg with taps from your schooling whip.

The very instant he moves, stop your aids. This is essential so that he associates moving off with the cessation of pressure or irritation (your aids). After several seconds, ask for halt (keep your seat still instead of accompanying his movements, and still your hands). Keep the aid on till he stops and if he does not do so, intensify it — close your thighs and resist *but never pull back* with your hands, and say whatever he responds to for stopping (I use 'Stand'). Again, the *instant* he stops cease the aids and praise him.

Repeat this process until he responds at once to your aids, and you should find that the habit of responding transfers to other aids, whether in the saddle, on the ground or in the stable. Always start with very light aids, intensifying if necessary, but reverting to light aids when responsiveness is improved.

From a schooling viewpoint, horses who are truly 'forward' rarely or never buck. An established rhythm with the habit of going forward as an attitude of mind will put paid to this potentially dangerous habit, provided the horse is not frightened or in discomfort or pain.

Relaxation

Relaxation is your starting point when using the Scales of Training. Given correct technique and empathy, relaxed, controlled riders produce relaxed controlled horses.

WHAT IS IT?

Relaxation is the prime quality needed for any rider and any horse, to ensure that everything that follows can be successfully performed. It is also often referred to as **looseness** and **suppleness** (which, for our purposes, are the same thing) – the opposite of stiffness, tension and those things that cause them.

These are:

- fear or nervousness, because of discomfort or pain, or the process of being ridden
- constraint and lack of correct physical exercises and work to stretch, strengthen and 'loosen up' tissues and joints, and
- asking the horse to perform movements he is not ready for and in a way he does not understand.

A relaxed horse is quiet (this does not mean dull or unresponsive and not interested in life). He is not upset by things going on around him.

SIGNS OF RELAXATION IN THE HORSE ARE:

- back, hindquarters and dock swinging from side to side in his gaits
- no pulling (unless his rider pulls at him, which is bad riding)
- snorting or high-blowing during his work
- a softly closed mouth with no excessive froth or drooling saliva, both signs of distress as well as of mouth problems (sharp, uneven teeth, sharp edges, an uncomfortable or harshly used bit and being held in tightly or into an outline). Drooling and frothing also occur when the horse's head and neck are held up and in, cramping his throat, so that he cannot swallow his saliva
- playing gently with the bit but not champing at it

A horse not swinging in his back or tracking-up. His back is down and his hind legs trailing.
After warming up, this experienced performance horse will loosen up, drop his head and neck, raise his back and engage his hindquarters.

- a relaxed facial expression and soft eye, looseness around the poll and ears, expressing interest but not over-excited or worried
- a naturally held head and neck (not up and tight) with the horse ready and happy to stretch his head and neck down and out in walk, trot and canter
- an even, confident stride
- smooth transitions with no raising of the head and neck
- the horse 'letting go' of his muscles and joints, allowing himself to flow
- the horse easily accepting his rider's aids and being easy to position.

SIGNS OF RELAXATION IN THE RIDER ARE:

- no fear: being afraid will tense you up more quickly than anything else
- sitting softly upright with the seat and legs around the horse, with loose seat and thigh muscles
- no tension in the neck and shoulders, riding with the latter gently pushed back and down, letting the upper arms drop naturally vertically and keeping the elbows skimming the hip bones
- not making tense facial expressions while riding

This rider is sitting in a very quiet, compliant seat, but her highly strung horse, despite having all the ridden freedom in the world, is rather tense and not as relaxed as his rider. This can be seen from his facial expression and the attitude of his head and neck.

Hold the reins softly, like this, with most of your hold between the thumb and index finger. This leaves your lower fingers free to use the reins. Do not feel that you need a hard, rigid grip on the reins; this is contrary to equestrian tact and good horsemanship.

- no clamping of the hands into fists, turning them into the stomach, gripping the reins hard or pulling on the horse's mouth
- letting the weight drop down through the heels rather than tensing the ankles
- concentrating on riding – not work, children, shopping lists or anything else
- giving smooth, consistent and correctly-timed aids as lightly as will get a result
- moving easily and minimally with the horse so as not to disturb his balance
- breathing deeply and smoothly
- sitting up proudly, straight, in control of the upper body and in balance with the horse.

A straight, balanced and symmetrical seat, with even weight on both seat bones and in both stirrups.

ASSESSING AND IMPROVING RELAXATION

An 'eye on the ground' can be invaluable, whether it is that of a good teacher or a knowledgeable friend. It is all too easy to get into bad habits. Also a ground observer has the great advantage of being able to see the horse's facial expression, which is an excellent guide to what he is thinking!

Go through the signs of relaxation for horse and rider on pages 18 and 19 slowly and with consideration, accepting honestly where either of you is lacking. Absence of any of the signs of relaxation is, rather obviously, an indication that that particular area needs attention.

It helps to do this a second time with the help of a good teacher or a knowledgeable friend who will tell you the truth – good or bad – about you and your horse. No one is all good or all bad, and you need to know it all in order to be able to improve.

YOUR HORSE

If you feel any unpleasant sensations when riding it will usually be due to lack of relaxation. Horses without a rider are normally at ease with their world provided they are not in pain, wearing uncomfortable clothing or unhappy with their situation. Therefore, when riding a healthy, sound horse, any disagreeable feelings such as jerkiness, hardness, resistance, unresponsiveness and so on could easily be due to lack of relaxation. But, of course, it goes deeper than that. You need to find out *why* your horse is not relaxed.

Tack

A major reason for tension is uncomfortable tack – a saddle that does not fit, a girth that causes discomfort or pain, a bridle and bit that are too tight or harshly used, or a training aid that forces a horse into the required posture, will all command your horse's attention above all else (other than directly life-threatening situations).

Saddles: the basic saddle-fit advice obviously holds true – you should be able to slide the flat of your fingers all around under the edges of the saddle fairly easily and try to check that the pressure seems fairly even. The saddle must be placed *behind* the tops of the shoulders at the sides of the withers so as not to discourage their use, and extend no further than the horse's last rib at the back. The traditional three fingers' width should be possible between the pommel and the withers, except with some close-contact jumping saddles, which need expert fitting. If the saddle is too narrow or too low over the spine and withers it will pinch; if too wide, it will rock: in both cases it will cause bruising and pain.

Girths: the girth must be smooth and comfortable. It must come at least a hand's width behind the point of the elbow to prevent its digging in here when the horse's foreleg comes back, causing bruising and discouraging free movement. It should have the facility to expand, usually by having elastic inserts at both ends or in the middle, so that there is no uneven pull on the saddle as the horse breathes. In my experience, girth materials that claim to have 'give' in them usually do not, and they restrict the horse's breathing. The girth should be only tight enough to keep the saddle in place and, generally, you should be able to slide the flat of your fingers underneath it, without pulling it away from your horse's side.

It is important to pull out your horse's forelegs carefully to smooth out the skin under the girth. Do not exaggerate this and take the leg out too far and too high: just enough to smooth out the skin without creating a pull anywhere is what you need.

Numnahs and pads: these must increase the horse's comfort, not be prone to wrinkling or slipping in use or be so small that their edges come beneath the saddle and cause pressure. They must be lifted well up into the saddle gullet to avoid pressure, especially on the withers. They can be either absorbent or designed to draw moisture away from the horse's back, and the same goes for girths. You can check that they are working by the state of the fabric after use. This is also a good guide to even or uneven pressure on the back, shown by the areas of sweat or grease on the numnah.

Your horse's back: if your horse's back shows rubbed hair immediately after removal of the saddle, it is causing friction. If, say, half an hour after removal, soft lumps appear, it is causing pressure. In both cases, it needs correcting. If you can actually feel a hollow in your horse's skin or muscles in the saddle area, the saddle is certainly exerting too much pressure there. Similar remarks apply to girths. Use a qualified saddle fitter to fit and check the fit of your horse's saddle and the shape of his back. This is especially important after a break, and as the horse gets fitter and more muscled up. Horses with uneven muscle development need remedial work and a specially fitted saddle.

Bridles: you should be able to run a finger easily under all parts of your bridle. The headpiece must not press into the backs of the horse's ears, nor the browband be so short that it causes this nor so long that it flops up and down. The throatlatch should be loose enough to allow the width of your hand between it and the round jawbone, otherwise the horse will sense that it is close to his throat and this alone will be enough to prevent him flexing to the bit, causing stiffness and tension.

This saddle is correctly placed, far enough back so that it does not interfere with the action of the shoulders, and so that the girth lies back from the elbows and will not dig in or interfere with his action, when he brings his forelegs back.

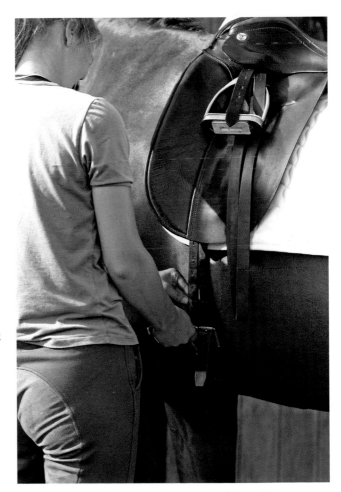

It is important for both safety and performance to check that tack fits comfortably. If a horse is uncomfortable his mind will concentrate on that. It will discourage or prevent him moving normally and well and, with some horses, can cause them to play up.

Nosebands: tight nosebands, one of the scourges of modern riding, dramatic though that sounds, also need to allow you to pass a finger easily under all parts of them, *including* over the bridge of the nose, not to mention around the bit and under the jaw or chin groove. The horse has to be able to slightly flex his jaw joints just below his ears in order to 'loosen' his mouth and play gently with the bit, and he cannot do that if his jaws are clamped shut. (See photos on page 90).

Bits: high bits cause horses a lot of misery and lead directly to tension and distress. Again, they are very common today. (For more details about different bits and their use and fitting see Chapter 3, Contact.)

Regarding the current fashion for using a bit needing a curb chain with a noseband involving a strap in the chin groove, this indicates that a horse is not controllable without significant constraint and is, therefore, bound to be a long way from relaxed. This is often due to 'strong' riding and rushed training, as well as hand- rather than seat-orientated methods (sustained, significant contact, pulling by the rider). Remedial schooling according to modern equine learning theory would greatly help such horses, riders and trainers.

Common faults seen in riding today are nosebands that are too high (rubbing the facial bones) and far too tight. Whatever type of noseband you choose to use, make sure that it is well fitted to allow your horse to relax properly and work at his best.

Sky's curb chain lies correctly, well down in his chin/curb groove. He does not wear a cover or a lip strap. Many people find that a lip strap can adversely affect the position and movement of the chain.

THE RIDER

Inconsiderate, unbalanced, harsh and generally poor riding are prime causes of lack of relaxation in horses. Indeed, they actively cause tension. Horses, like us, brace themselves against pain, discomfort or unbalanced weight. If we have an uncomfortable pair of shoes or boots, we alter our way of walking to try to lessen the pain or discomfort. If the horse's movement is made difficult or painful by his rider (or tack, as described), he will move differently from his normal gait to try to escape it, and concentrate on this rather than on his work. This causes the development of the muscles used in this impeded movement rather than those that would be used when moving correctly and which are obvious in a well-ridden and well-schooled (and, therefore, correctly developed) horse.

Similarly, if the rider's weight is persistently out of balance with the horse, such as in a rider who usually sits more heavily or tilted to one side, collapsed sideways at waist or hip, with one shoulder or hand higher than the other, with her head tilted to one side or with uneven hip openness, the horse will brace against this uncomfortable force and pressure. The rider may not realize that she is sitting in this way and that it is not only affecting the sensations she transmits to her horse but also the precise messages she is giving her horse. These messages will almost certainly be uneven in pressure and/or position and will be giving the horse signals the rider does not intend. Then, when the horse does his best to comply with the signals he perceives, he will not give the rider the response she wants or expects. This can result in correction, punishment, tension, a more firmly applied aid (giving an even stronger, but similar aid), anxiety and confusion in the horse and frustration and even anger in the rider. Of course, all this completely blocks relaxation, looseness or suppleness in both of you.

This is not a book on riding technique, as explained earlier. Books on that important subject are listed under Further Reading on page 150. A combination of reading and study, lessons from a good teacher and practice are the way to improve riding technique so that you help your horse as much as possible, and are not the cause of tension.

If your teacher or a knowledgeable friend points out that you have a physical fault, such as lack of straightness or balance, that you cannot seem to correct when riding, it is well worth consulting a human physical therapist of some kind, such as a physiotherapist or sports massage therapist, because until it is sorted out you and your horse will both be working at a significant disadvantage.

Walking on a completely loose, free rein like this is a fairly sure-fire way of relaxing a horse, particularly if the rider can steel herself to do nothing meanwhile! One of the hardest things to do on a horse is nothing. Frequent breaks like this, every few minutes, are very important in refreshing, relaxing and calming a horse.

MANAGEMENT

Feeding: a great deal of poor behaviour in horses is caused by inappropriate feeding. Feeds that are high in cereal starch can cause excitable behaviour. In some horses and ponies only a small amount is needed to set them off, but other horses can take more generous quantities. However, nutritionists now recommend that we provide our horses' energy requirements from high-energy fibrous feeds, if they are working hard, rather than cereals. The latter are fed in smaller amounts than previously.

Buyers are often confused by the words 'cool', 'non-heating' and 'calm' on bags of feed, but these do not mean that they are cereal free. Check the ingredients list and if you see any kind of grain at all listed there – oats, barley, maize/corn, or even wheat or rye, depending on where you live – you will know that it contains cereal. Try to do without cereal if your horse tends to be highly strung or tense; experiment with different diets and quantities. Lack of sufficient forage (fibre such as hay, haylage and short-chopped forage feeds) can cause digestive discomfort and a tense, unhappy horse. Don't forget lots of clean, fresh water.

Take advice from the nutritionist at the company whose feeds you use. Try to get your horse on a settled but flexible diet that works for him, makes him comfortable inside, does not hype him up and he likes.

Remember as well, that nearly all horses live for grass, the food they were meant to live on. Don't underestimate its importance to your horse and give him as much time grazing as you can, bearing in mind health considerations. This really calms most horses.

Daily routine: it is often said that horses are creatures of habit and like a settled routine. This can certainly be so, but even more important is that the horse associates his surroundings and his companions – human, equine and anything else – with pleasure and safety. Horses want to feel comfortable and safe, otherwise they *will* feel tense. Tense horses are running constantly in a slight 'flight-or-fight' state: this is not good for them and, in fact, is bad horse-care practice.

Horses need congenial company (not being forced to be near those they do not like), good shelter, somewhere dry and comfortable to lie and rest, no more clothing

All horses really want to do is graze with their family and friends. In domestic situations, grazing sometimes has to be restricted, but it should still form a regular, preferably daily, part of a horse's care.

This young gelding, Comberton Clancy, is quite highly strung and sensitive but is fortunate enough to be in the ownership of his home stud, Comberton Stud, and ridden by its owner, Sally Hobbs, who is a highly skilled and tactful rider. Relaxation is sometimes a problem for Clancy and one dreads to think how he would be with a more forceful rider.

than absolutely necessary (and very well-fitting, light and comfortable), the security of ample food and water, and plenty of freedom to be turned out and do horsey things like rolling, galloping around, playing and socializing with friends. Horses with this kind of lifestyle are always more relaxed and calm than those deprived of these basic requirements.

Treatment: the way you handle and generally maintain your horse has a great capacity to keep him relaxed and content. Things you can do in this regard are sensitive grooming that does not irritate him, keeping his skin comfortable and his hooves properly trimmed and, if necessary, shod so that he is confident and comfortable in his feet, keeping his body toned and supple by means of massage, hand-rubbing and stretching and maybe treatments such as an aromatherapy massage or a shiatsu session.

Rise above the ordinary in your care of your horse and you will definitely notice a rewarding difference in a contented, settled and calm horse. Even those with highly strung or nervous temperaments relax more easily when they are confident in their care.

Carefully stretching your horse's legs both forwards and backwards helps loosen him up before work. With the forelegs, make sure you lift them from the knee and then ask for the full stretch. Some practitioners prefer to support the legs by holding one hand under the knee or hock, as well, for safety and the horse's comfort.

YOURSELF

If you are naturally a tense person it will initially be difficult for you to ride in a relaxed way, but there is plenty you can do for yourself to calm down – if you really want to. Although you cannot change your temperament you can alter its effect on you by getting things into proportion, maybe adjusting your attitude to the various elements of your life, and by not spreading yourself too thinly in relation to the things you take on.

I find that tense people very often go 'over the top' in everything they do, and sometimes this is due to a feeling of personal insecurity for which there is no need. They also tend to be impatient (the last thing a rider needs), changeable and inconsistent (again, not good qualities for a horse person). It is usually a good plan to try to take a more laid-back attitude to everything and to consider that if you don't, not only will you not achieve your equestrian goals, whatever they may be, but also you will be adversely affecting your horse's wellbeing which, in turn, will make it very difficult for him to relax.

A highly strung, tense rider would do well to get a particularly laid-back, calm and quiet horse, but not a slug – which could irritate her even more. Tense riders and tense horses do not make good partnerships, but if you have your horse already and do not wish to part with him, try the various suggestions given here for both him and yourself.

Take the time to look after yourself and give yourself some real pleasure in relaxing pursuits, wear really comfortable clothes that make you feel good when you are 'off duty', get plenty of sound sleep, have a professional massage now and then, and cultivate the ability to say a firm 'No' when people try to make demands on you. Above all don't be a perfectionist because, if you are, you will never be really happy and relaxed.

You might find my book *The Horse Owner's Essential Survival Guide* useful too (see page 150). It is full of ideas on how to cut corners in horse management without compromising your horse, and save time and money. Plenty of people have told me that it is a great attitude adjuster: this makes for greater self-confidence and, consequently, contentment and relaxation.

Depending on your horse's temperament, standing still to chat can calm him down or irritate him – usually the former after a period of work. If the latter, keep your seat and leg muscles relaxed, stroke the horse (this is more calming than patting) just in front of his withers and use your voice to relax him.

Lack of relaxation in riders is often shown by raised, stiff shoulders, rigid hands and contact, tense face and jaw and stiff legs – although hopefully not all in the same person!

The exercises shown here are standard for helping riders relax before riding, but very few people actually take the time or trouble to perform them before riding. Making your body move in a way that carefully loosens and stretches its soft tissues and joints is not difficult or painful. The trick is not to force any movement. Perform each one three times, the first time with no 'push' at all, the second time just pushing it a little and the third time taking the movement to its extreme point *without* in any way approaching the point where you feel significant pain. Releasing stiffness may feel slightly uncomfortable, but if you reach the point where you feel like saying 'Ouch!' you've overdone it. This can cause injury, which is counterproductive.

People who do not habitually exercise in a structured way also often rush the job because they think it is a waste of time, really. Take it seriously and think of it as benefiting yourself and your riding and, therefore, your horse too.

Stand on a step or step ladder making sure you are in good balance, with your toes on the step and your heels free. Drop your heels down gently to give the backs of your legs and your ankles a good stretch, then move on to tiptoes to loosen up your toes and ankles. Don't be tempted to bounce as you might overstretch the tissues.

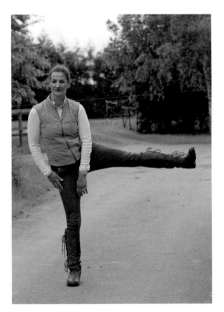

See if you can lift your legs horizontally to the side – excellent for hip joint and general groin suppleness. Alice is obviously not only supple but well balanced, as she holds these poses for our photographer.

Carefully swinging your legs straight forward and back works your hip joints, and also helps to improve your balance generally.

PROBLEMS DUE TO LACK OF RELAXATION

The reason that Relaxation is placed by many as the foundation stone of the Scales of Training is because it affects everything. Lack of it creates tension, distraction, anxiety, stiffness, a heightening of the horse's flight-or-fight instinct, a possible raising of the rider's fear level and, quite simply, poor performance and lack of progress.

As a prey animal, the horse relies on his flight instinct for survival. There is nothing he can do about this. It is a well-ingrained instinct. Some horses are more easily frightened or worried than others, but even a slight raising of his anxiety level is bad news.

We hear a lot about the presence of gastric ulcers in horses who are stabled for long periods and/or fed insufficient fibre (hay, haylage or forage feed) but I feel that another trigger for the development of ulcers, as in people, is the frequent experiencing of situations that raise the horse's alarm levels and trigger the production of adrenaline, which stimulates him to flee. People living or working in stressful situations frequently suffer from indigestion. This can be an early-warning sign that all is not right and can develop into gastric ulcers. It is reasonable to suppose that this applies to other animals as well.

So, it is not only the horse's work and schooling that are badly affected by lack of relaxation, but also his very wellbeing, particularly if his management is also not appropriate for him as an individual.

Plenty of time off in the field goes a long way towards keeping the horse mentally stable and exercising his own body in ways that we can't.

TECHNIQUES TO HELP FIND RELAXATION

Your own demeanour around your horse is crucial: you need to appear calm, strong, confident and quiet, even if you don't entirely feel it. Horses quickly pick up on how we are feeling. They also hate being rushed, so, although you may be in a hurry to get your horse done and dusted so that you can go and do whatever else you have to do, it is not the best approach to adopt.

Learn the busy person's important skill of time management: prioritize and apportion your time so that you have plenty of time to care for and ride your horse, and keep your mind on him as you do so. Don't give much time at all to things that aren't important to you. Also, decide for yourself what is important, as other people are often all too keen to take your time and can be very good at making you think you should give it! Probably, your family and animals, and your closest friends are the centre of your world, but only you can make that decision.

Learn basic massage and hand-rubbing techniques: once your horse is used to you doing these things for him sensitively and reassuringly, he will calm down and munch his haynet while you do them and enjoy the routine. Horses massage each other during mutual grooming, and it is known that it lowers their heart rate. Something as simple as firm but sensitive and unhurried stroking all over his body with the flat of your hands (upwards on the legs then a downward stroke to lay the hair as you finish) is enough to calm and relax him. (For more details on this technique see *Know Your Horse Inside Out*, listed under Further Reading on page 150).

Learn as much as you can about horse care and management: horses need freedom, company, shelter, somewhere comfortable to lie and rest, and protection from insects and too-hot or too-cold surroundings. Over-rugging is another modern failing that makes thousands of horses miserable and can cause overheating. Many horses today are fed far too many cereals, when most of them need hardly any. Cereals do have a place in the diets of genuinely hard-working horses or others who find it hard to maintain their weight (check teeth and worming status), but most do much better on a low to moderate energy fibrous feed. Too many cereals and too much energy from any source are prime causes of lack of relaxation.

When massaging your horse use firm, smooth strokes and lean your weight into him. Start at his neck and then continue down his body, giving a little more concentration and using a little more pressure on muscular areas.

The rider has just put more weight on to her left seat bone and down into her left stirrup to start changing from right flexion and direction to left.

Check your riding techniques: relaxed seat and leg muscles (which many people do not have today) plus toned control of your upper body muscles and position are the basis of a good riding position. Constantly tell yourself to stay loose in the seat, to hold your spine and head upright and let your upper arms drop naturally down so that your elbows are almost always by your hips. Riding with your elbows forwards and with short reins on a significant contact is bound to hype up many horses, even slightly, and is bad riding practice. You don't want this.

Keep working sessions short: do not expect your horse to work and concentrate intensively for more than a very few minutes (no more than ten) at a time. Then give a couple of minutes either walking calmly on a loose rein (on the buckle) or just standing still with complete freedom to stretch, so make sure your reins are long enough to allow this; if they aren't, buy a longer pair. Finish after something good and walk on a loose rein, ideally in-hand with a loosened girth and run-up stirrups, to cool, calm and relax your horse.

Correct rushing by using tactful half-halts and large, loose circles, turns and changes of direction: bring your horse down to the gait below the one in which he rushed for seven to ten seconds, then resume the previous gait. When jumping, use this technique for horses who rush between fences or in the approach. Do not jump until he is calm. Rushing can be a sign of anxiety or fear in horses. If your

The light seat: just a slight lift of the seat and forward angle to the upper body. The back remains flat, a stronger posture than a crouched, rounded position.

Being able to control your horse's feet and get him to stand still disengages the flight-or-fight process in his brain and you can start again, calmly, in several seconds.

horse rushes frequently, bring him gently to halt and make him stand with his feet still and head down for about ten seconds or longer, then start again. (See page 35 for how to do this.) This calms him and 'disengages' the flight-or-fight response in his brain: the more he rushes and fidgets the more he will do it since it becomes a habit. Horses form habits very easily, good ones and bad.

Use selected words and the tone of your voice to stimulate, calm or correct your horse: horses do respond to the human voice and it is an invaluable and under-used aid – but don't chatter to him. Accompany praise with a stroke (not pat) on his neck, as this, too, is calming. Patting and thumping are not, even though a rider may think that she is expressing her pleasure to the horse.

A very forward position: mainly used for fast work. Being too far forward reduces the rider's security should the horse suddenly deviate from his course.

A useful seat for general cross-country riding: the seat is lifted more and the upper body angled more forward.

EXERCISES

Techniques and exercises to teach and promote relaxation are a valuable part of your horse-skills knowledge. You may need to use them regularly with some horses, and all horses can benefit from them after work.

VOICE AIDS

One of the most valuable techniques you can learn in handling, managing, riding and schooling your horse is the correct use of voice aids. There are two main problems that I come across when teaching clients, or just being with them as they prepare for a lesson or see to their horse afterwards.

1. *Tending to chat to their horses*: this is fine if it is intended to give your horse a clear message as to your mood, although he will probably pick up on that anyway. Otherwise, this is not the best way to give him an aid with a view to getting a response. Horses often do pick out individual words and act according to what they associate them with but, for effective communication, simple, clear words or sounds are best. Also, some

people, when they want to correct their horse, often use rather sarcastic language in a complete sentence, as if they genuinely think that the horse can understand it. Of course, he cannot.

2. *Hardly using their voices at all:* this is because the voice is not allowed in most dressage tests! I cannot understand the logic of this line of thought in a training situation however. The voice is an effective and priceless technique when schooling and also in other forms of riding, and I strongly believe that it is foolish not to make the best use of it. It helps the horse, when used properly and clearly in a way that he can understand, and anything we can do to help our horses should be done.

The flight-or-fight mechanism is a horse's prime survival technique, hard-wired into him over many millions of years. Under saddle it can cause problems, so you need to make relaxation a primary requirement and learn how to instil it.

Schooling to the voice

Horses need at least a basic vocabulary of 'Stand', 'Over', 'Head down', 'Walk on', 'Ter-rot' *or* 'Trot on' (not both as they sound different), 'Can-ter' and 'Back'. I also want horses to understand 'Good boy/girl' or 'There!' in a pleased tone of voice, and 'No' in a sterner tone of voice. I realize that some trainers do not feel that horses understand what we mean by these sounds, but my experience is that they do. Many people use the sound 'Whoa', often long drawn-out, to slow or stop a horse. With horses trained in Iberia or by Iberian trainers, the sound 'Aaaahhhh', low-pitched, usually secures a slow, stop and relaxation. I use a long drawn-out 'Easy' to calm down a horse who is getting over-excited or going too fast within a particular gait and, again, this is understood by most in my experience.

The horse must associate the sound with the movement (or lack of it) that you want. The voice aid for any movement is best introduced as soon as the horse is obeying the physical aid. As with teaching anything, the horse has to be calm and paying you attention before an actual command can be effective.

Most horses learn voice commands during training in-hand and on the lunge, but as soon as they are ridden people often stop using them. A horse does not forget, though, and will soon pick up or learn new ones if you cannot find out what words or sounds he learnt earlier.

EXERCISE 1 – TEACHING VOICE COMMANDS

- *It is often easier to start in-hand. Hold your lead rope, look ahead and start walking, then, as soon as he lifts a foot to go with you, say 'Walk on'. If you are riding your horse and you want him to walk, give the physical aid (say, a squeeze or tap with your leg or a nudge with your seat). As he starts to walk stop your physical aid, so that he links complying with the removal of the pressure of your aid.*
- *After two seconds, say 'Walk on' so that he associates the sound with the movement.*
- *When you come to a halt, as soon as his feet are still say 'stand' so that, again, he associates still feet with 'stand'.*
- *After a few successful tries, you can give him the vocal aid a split second after the physical aid has been released, and he will comply.*

If you can control your horse's feet you have control of your horse. Therefore, obedience to the command 'Stand' and being able to slow your horse down or stop him is essential to obtaining cooperation in-hand or under saddle. It is also a great safety feature, of course. (For details on how to achieve this, see page 36.)

Two techniques that help to lower a horse's heart rate and, therefore, calm and relax him, are asking him to lower his head on a long rein or lead rope and rubbing his neck just in front of the withers, where horses mutually groom each other.

A lovely picture of relaxed, considerate lungeing. The horse is wearing no tight gadgets, he is clearly calm and well-balanced and going well within himself. His trainer is herself walking with him on a large circle to give him as much freedom as possible.

EXERCISE 2 – ASK THE HORSE TO LOWER HIS HEAD

- *Have a tidbit in the hand not holding the lead rope, let the horse smell it and lower your hand to the ground.*
- *His head will almost certainly follow and, as it does, say 'Head down' and give him the treat when the head is down.*
- *You can get the same effect with many horses by simply pointing to the ground, but the food treat method works better.*
- *When the movement becomes reliable, you do not always need the treat and can use the command successfully from ground or saddle.*

Stroking and patting

It is always better to stroke your horse than pat him as a 'reward'. The inverted commas are there because many people feel that horses do not understand the concept of reward as we do. Horses do know, though, whether we are pleased or not, and seem to relax when neck and withers stroking is accompanied by a vocal reward or calming signal such as 'Good boy'. Patting is a short, sharp sensation equivalent to being nipped and sent away by another horse in herd life, and so is not a good technique to use for calming a horse or for praising or rewarding him, come to that. It is particularly inappropriate when it actually becomes a hard slap or a thump, as used by some riders after a horse has done well in a competition, when the horse has no concept of it and, according to equine mores, is being told 'Go away, I don't want you!'

Stroking the area around a horse's withers is proven to lower his heart rate (one of the benefits of mutual grooming) so is excellent for calming and relaxing a horse, especially combined with the loose rein.

RIDING FOR RELAXATION

Some riders find it very difficult to truly relax on a horse, even when the horse could be called a patent safety ride. The techniques given here have proved themselves many times in practice and are well worth learning about.

EXERCISE 3 – A SAFETY VALVE

First of all, it helps if you have a failsafe trick up your sleeve to calm down an excited horse, so try this. My classical trainer of the 80s, Desi Lorent, trained all his horses to stop what they were doing immediately their rider gave them a long stroke down the left side of the neck. They clearly took this to mean 'Stop work' and, no matter how hyped up some of his pretty sensitive horses had become under a clumsy, novice or not-so-novice rider, they switched off like a light and walked calmly or stood still. This was another great safety feature. I never asked Desi how he taught it, but I find that the following works:

- *if your horse becomes genuinely upset, immediately stop all your aids and sit still and relaxed*
- *at the same time, give one long stroke down one side of the neck (always the same side so that your horse associates that specific feel with you relaxing and work stopping)*
- *either stand, or walk, relaxed on a loose, free rein. Your horse will soon make the connection between your physical signals (relaxation and stroke) and no demands being made on him.*

This also works if the horse becomes startled by something beyond your control, such as a frightening experience outside the arena or when hacking.

EXERCISE 4 – RELAXATION, STRAIGHTNESS AND BALANCE – YOU, THAT IS

Check that your horse is comfortable before you start.

- *Make sure that the bridle is not irritating him, the headpiece not pressing in behind his ears, buckles not rubbing his eyes, the throatlatch loose enough to fit the width of your hand between it and his round jawbone and the noseband loose enough for you to be able to easily slide a finger all around it under the straps.*
- *The bit/s should be fitted as described on page 89.*
- *Remind yourself to ride with relaxed seat and leg muscles and to sit up with a toned upper body and dropped upper arms. Make sure that you are sitting straight and in balance with no tension.*

Whether you are going into the manege or for a hack, you should start by walking on as loose a rein as you dare, depending on circumstances, for five or ten minutes.

EXERCISE 5 – CONTROL HIS FEET

Controlling his feet so that complying becomes a habit with your horse also helps to control any unwanted behaviours such as charging off, bucking, shying and general messing about. These are all part of the horse's flight-or-fight and avoidance response and are instinctive and well-established in the horse, since flight is his main survival technique. The more a horse uses this response, which involves fast use of his feet, the more it becomes a habit and such behaviour becomes worse. Therefore, with a strong 'stand' habit in place (the more you do it, the more habitual it becomes) you have easier control. Still his feet, wait six or seven seconds, then move off again.

It is often said that we should 'ride a horse through' unwanted behaviours such as those described above and 'make use of the energy' he expends performing them, but doing that does not slow or stop his feet. Those techniques can, in practice, correct him to some extent but not so effectively as stopping him performing them by transitioning to a lower gait or stopping, because this works with his psychological make-up and has surer, long-term effects. For this reason, do not keep riding him around to 'settle' him but instead control his feet.

- If your horse is not calm but is messing about, halt and command 'Stand' in a quiet, authoritative tone.
- Immediately he does so and keeps his feet still, say 'Good boy'.
- If he moves without your aid, even just lifting a foot, give your halt aid and say 'No' firmly but without raising your voice, which would hype him up more.
- If he continues to move, give the aid for halt, then command 'Stand' without in any way indicating tenseness or fear in your voice.
- As soon as his feet are still stop the aid.
- Wait for six or seven seconds, then ask him to walk.
- Use clear, simple words, which he probably already knows, and time them correctly.

THE ESSENTIAL FREE REIN

It is very important that horses learn to go in self-balance on a free and loose rein in all gaits early in their training, as this promotes agility and self-control.

Warm-up in walk

- Assuming that your horse is calm enough to begin his session walking on a loose rein, do this for five or ten minutes. Don't make the common mistakes of immediately bringing your horse 'into an outline', or starting trot work within two or three circuits of the school or after only a few hundred metres out hacking. Like any athlete, your horse needs to work on limbering up first to increase his circulation and loosen up his joints and tissues. He needs to stride out freely with his head and neck relaxed and swinging (like his back and dock).

Turning

- Guide him with your seat, weight and leg aids. Generally, where you put your weight your horse will go: slightly weighting one seat bone more than its partner will encourage the horse to go that way to maintain his balance naturally.

Large-diameter curved tracks in rising trot help a horse to relax, soften his head and neck and start to push forwards and swing along.

- Use your outside leg in a sideways on-off squeezing or tapping aid to 'push' him away from the pressure around curves, stopping the aid the instant he complies so that he associates the movement he has just made with the stopping of the aid, and learns that he has given the correct response.
- Light outside rein pressure sideways against the lower part of his neck will also help to turn him, or even just a push on the outside of his withers with your outside hand. Again, stop aiding the instant he complies.

Trotting

- When you start trotting, just give the aid to trot and stop it as soon as he does. Using your legs at every stride, as is often taught, creates a dull, insensitive, confused horse who eventually ignores your legs.
- Use a relaxed rising trot at first and immediately quell any tendency to go too fast by using your slow-down aid, and also by timing your rise to the speed you want to go. In your mind, think 'slow' and work on a limbering-up, relaxed, striding-out trot.

Creating energy

- If you have the opposite problem of insufficient forward movement, work on forwardness as described in the previous chapter. Encourage him happily, not in a telling-off kind of way.
- You must start with the lightest leg-taps or squeezes and increase their pressure, possibly accompanied by taps (only taps) with your schooling whip just behind your leg or, if strictly necessary, further back to stimulate his hind legs, until you get the response you want, then stop the aid and let him carry you round.
- If you have given him a vocal aid, do not repeat it once he is trotting, but use a different sound such as tongue clicks to encourage more energy from him if he is slugging along. The instant you get the response you want, stop the aid and say 'Good boy' in a pleased tone.

Using light seat in canter on large curves is helping to calm Clancy, who is starting to soften in his jaw and neck and to engage his hindquarters, pushing energetically along.

Canter

- The same principles are used to canter as in the other gaits – light rein, relaxed seat, controlled upper body.
- Keep your inside seat bone and shoulder slightly forward in canter, even on a straight line, in accordance with whichever leg he is leading with – for right lead, put your right seat bone and shoulder a little forward, and vice versa. This not only warns him that you are going to ask for canter but instructs him to stay in canter until you put the shoulder and seat bone back level with their pairs again, when your horse will trot.
- That is all the aid you need. Stay relaxed so that only this message is reaching your horse, and he will also stay relaxed and obey easily.

- This position aid seems to be naturally understood by horses at once, other than those who have not been allowed any initiative in how they go.
- With these, just relax your mind, seat and legs. Maintain a light bit contact, give a clear warning of your intention to canter by putting the inside side of your body forward, as described above, for one or two strides of sitting trot or walk, then give your aid – maybe outside leg back from the hip (not the knee) and squeeze or tap, preferably when the outside hind is lifting as this is the one that starts the canter stride.
- Remember that if you give your aid when the foot is on the ground he cannot comply immediately as the foot is rooted – it normally just results in a slightly delayed reaction which, longer term, reduces lightness and forwardness a little.

Shallow loops with correct change of flexion and bend are good for developing a supple body, particularly if the policy is followed to encourage self-balance in the horse. Here, Clancy maintains his posture under Sally's light, guiding hand and easily changes flexion and bend.

Too much speed

- We are still in our 'free rein' time, so keep your balance upright and use your voice, seat and thighs (to 'hug' the horse) if he goes too fast, with a light rein contact.
- If you have a definite inkling that he is going to go too fast, take up more contact particularly with the outside rein and aid him to slow down, or come to a halt if he is getting too onward bound. This controls his feet, remember. Six or seven strides in a lower gait (trot or walk) or six or seven seconds standing still will 'disconnect' the tendency to flight response he has just shown, and you can start again, calmly.

General tips

- Do not just go round and round the track, if schooling in a manege. Work on the inside track to discourage your horse from psychologically leaning on the fence for support, and only do one circuit of the school at a time, as nothing is more deadening (not relaxing) than going round and round on the track in the same direction.
- For warming up, use changes of rein and large circles, transitions – remembering to re-check your horse's stop-and-stand compliance now and then – and, when you feel he is warmed up and listening to you (say after about ten or fifteen minutes), give him a break by just standing still or walking calmly around on a free rein.

- Giving your horse well-timed, clear aids, not using hands and legs at precisely the same moment, and stopping the aids as soon as you get your response, all keep your horse relaxed by not confusing him. This is simple communication of the type horses understand so that they do not become upset and anxious.
- Whatever level of schooling your horse is at, frequent breaks of walking or standing on a completely loose rein will relax him. Keeping going for too long without a break will actually reduce the schooling progress, can be abusive to the horse as it can cause pain and fear and will have an adverse effect on his association with work and the place where it is carried out.
- The greener, weaker and more unfit the horse, the more frequent your breaks need to be. Even with a fit, schooled horse, do not work him without a break for more than five minutes.
- His body may be capable and physically fit but his mind is still, and always, that of a horse, and he finds concentration over a longer period difficult. Drilling and compulsive riding spoil a horse's associations and attitude and have no place in classical, modern, humane riding. If you are having a problem with a particular movement, do not go on and on pushing for it. Be happy with a good try, stop asking at once, praise the horse and give him a break. This is how to keep him confident, readily compliant and relaxed.

RIDING FOR LOOSENESS/SUPPLENESS

As your horse's schooling progresses, you will introduce various exercises into his sessions to work his joints and tissues and increase his looseness/suppleness and agility, all part of the Relaxation scale. Effective exercises are:

- transitions between walk and trot and trot and canter and back again (see page 61)
- using free gaits to encourage free, forward movement – medium walk and working trot.

Good transitions from trot to canter and back develop balance, strength and suppleness. In this change from trot to right canter, Clancy changes up while maintaining his posture and remaining balanced and calm.

In this sequence, Sally and Clancy are changing from left canter to trot (3). Clancy has maintained his head and neck posture and his engagement, and has transitioned to a forward-going trot, in self balance (7).

3

4

7

8

1

- use shallow corners that actually constitute part of a 10m circle, to allow for your horse's balance. If he shows any tendency to 'fall in', weight your outside stirrup, support with your inside thigh and give little vibrations or gentle squeezes on the inside rein to suggest that he looks around his circle

2

3

Changes of rein out of a circle or large curve call for the horse to balance himself while making his change of direction and without losing his correct posture. This needs and encourages suppleness and agility.

- change the rein fairly often to keep your horse interested and do not simply go round and round the school on the outside track – make large circles, loose serpentines and shallow loops (see diagrams below)
- turns on or about the forehand (see pages 50–51)
- leg yield (see pages 52–53)

A good 3-track shoulder-in with not too much bend and flexion in the head and neck – a common fault.

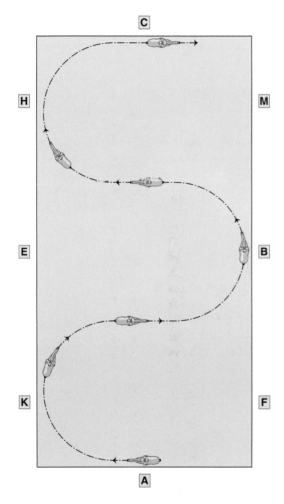

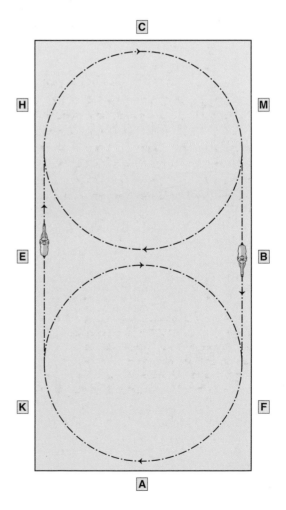

- shoulder-in and -out on the straight and on circles and spirals, as the horse progresses (see page 58)
- 20m circles initially in walk, then trot and, as the horse becomes more balanced, in canter in a light seat and then a 'school' seat. The horse can be spiralled down eventually to 10m circles when his strength and balance show that he is ready
- work over low poles, later raising them just a few inches or centimetres.

Thorney has a good try at walk pirouette for Emma, reaching well across with his right fore and remaining lightly in hand.

Understanding 'long and low'

One of the first things you need to understand is the way of going known as 'long and low', as a suppling and strengthening exercise, and a means of teaching the horse a safe weight-carrying posture. This involves encouraging the horse to go with the muscles along the underside of his neck, belly and hindquarters contracting to lift his spine, enhancing its natural slight upward arch, which is a strong, weight-carrying structure. This posture also encourages the lower part of the pelvis to tilt under by flexing/opening the lumbo-sacral joint sited at the croup. This brings forward the hind limbs, so that they are stepping further forward underneath the horse.

The outline the horse presents from the side is one of a rounded, lengthened topline and a lifted, shortened line along the underside of his belly, from elbows to stifles. His neck is arched forward, out and slightly down, and the front of his face is on or slightly in front of an imaginary vertical line dropped from his forehead to the ground. As a guide, he should be working with his poll level with or only slightly lower than his withers. His pelvis ('bottom') is tucked under and his hind legs brought further under his belly. His back and dock should be swinging in rhythm with his movement.

A relaxed walk on long-reins, the horse stretching down and walking out.

Coming more into hand, the horse trots on with good forward movement and a calm listening demeanour.

A good long-and-low performance. Personally, I would prefer to see the nose a little more in front of the vertical.

Achieving the long-and-low posture

This sounds all well and good, but how do you achieve this 'foundation' and beneficial way of going as a teaching tool and exercise for suppling and strengthening your horse? Many people do it with training aids, but mental and physical harm can be done if these are not applied properly.

It is quite possible to achieve the required posture by giving the horse a comfortable contact on the outside rein and an intermittent, 'feeling' one, as needed, on the inside one to ask him to yield to the pressure. Many horses do not even need this. When lungeing or long-reining your horse, there will be moments when he drops his muzzle towards the ground and this is the moment to say *'Good boy'* in a really pleased tone. He should understand this from your handling of him already. I have known *very* few horses who will not then catch on and repeat any movement you have praised.

Don't forget the 'Head down' command described earlier, which you may have taught him as part of general handling training. As he is familiar with it, you can give the command and, as he complies, say 'Good boy'. Because horses watch for and respond to our body language, this is another way to get your horse to lower his head and neck on the lunge. You simply lower your head and shoulders a little and lower the lungeing rein, and it is highly likely that he will lower his head and neck to mimic you. As always, praise him the instant he does so.

- When riding, establish a relaxed, confident rising trot – not so fast that the horse powers along and rushes out of balance – and give the horse a comfortable, hand-holding contact on the outside rein. This is your master rein, its main job being to help regulate the horse's speed.
- Encourage him with squeezes from your calves in time with his rhythm but do not give leg aids once he is going actively forward.
- To stimulate the hind legs if he is not responding, bring your legs back from the hips and give your

on-off squeezing or tapping aids, firmly maybe but not harshly, in the behind-the-girth position. Light taps with a schooling whip, in rhythm with your squeezes, can reinforce your leg aids if they are having no effect at all.

- As soon as he is moving reasonably forwardly and rhythmically – this is a young, green or unfit horse we are considering – praise him and stop your leg aid.
- Concentrate on giving your horse a rhythmic feel with your rise, which encourages him to swing along, and keep your gentle but noticeable contact on the outside rein with an even gentler (but 'there') contact on the inside one.
- As you give the gentle squeezes on the inside rein, give the command 'Head down', and, of course, cease the squeezes and the command the instant the horse complies. You must be very quick to release a little with the reins to allow this movement. If you are late in releasing the reins the horse will feel a resistance in his mouth as he does what you have asked. He will take this as your stopping him doing it, so you will have thoroughly confused him.
- As he achieves the posture you have asked for, say 'Good boy' again. Pretty soon, your horse will associate not only the 'Head down' command but also the gentle squeezes on the bit with yielding to the bit and lowering his head and neck. *This is not at all the same as sawing his head down with your hands. The association allows you to gently remind or ask him what you want, when appropriate, and you then have to allow it by releasing your contact (simply opening your lower three fingers should be enough) to the extent that he can adopt the posture without your contact pulling his muzzle in behind the vertical. Maintaining a gentle contact keeps your horse in horizontal balance so that he is not boring down on to either his mouth or his forelegs, which is potentially detrimental to his future schooling and development, and also to the soundness of his legs.*

Once this association is confirmed in his brain, whenever he is going in a hollow, 'sunken' outline despite your correct seat, leg and rhythmic movement, all you need do is give a gentle squeeze on the inside rein and/or the 'Head down' command to ask him to round down. The act of lowering the head and neck when moving brings up the back and belly and tucks under the hindquarters, bringing the hind legs forwards at the same time. This is exactly the reaction and posture you want at this stage of training, and to stretch and relax a more advanced horse later on.

Training aids

Often, training aids are adjusted too tightly, compelling the horse to go in a shortened, rather than a long outline (remember – *long* and low), with a 'squashed in' neck and with the front of the face firmly on or behind the vertical in the mistaken quest for quickly achieving 'roundness'. Also, many riders demand this way of going by over-firm bit pressure and a sawing action on the mouth, or by holding the head rigidly in the position they want it to assume.

This work is the subject of much misunderstanding and misuse. Asking the horse to work with the front of his face behind that vertical line severely restricts his vision because of the way his eyes work, and probably also disorientates him from a balance viewpoint because his balance mechanism is sited inside his ears. At least one internationally respected classical horseman has suggested that it could even make the horse feel physically sick due to sensory deprivation.

Although many people still use this 'over-rounded' posture, often with harshly adjusted and used training aids, increasingly administrative organizations and concerned individuals in equestrian sports hold the view, as was the case a couple of decades ago and before, that it is wrong, a mentally abusive way of forcing a horse to work and that it causes physical damage to the body.

'Long and low' is a necessary suppling and strengthening exercise because the opposite posture – with the top line and belly sagging down, the hind legs trailing and not engaged forward or able to push properly, and the neck and head sagging down and out – is a weak way for the horse to hold himself and, especially, to carry weight, and one in which he is likely to sustain stress injuries, particularly of his back. If the rider is trying to achieve a good posture only by means of the hands, pulling the head in and down, the back is also strained as the horse resists the discomfort.

Pole work

Even with quite green horses, put down the odd single pole and get him used to walking, trotting and maybe cantering over it for interest, depending on his attitude and likely reaction (think calm and relaxed), and to teach him to consider what he is doing with his feet. Leading him over a pole initially is a good plan; you are beside him, *looking ahead*, not at him, and he will almost certainly just go with you. Horses normally hate treading on poles and it can frighten them and put them off. Treat the whole thing in a relaxed way and do not approach the pole too quickly. Give him a loose rope so that he can look at the pole and gauge his own lift-up point; you decide the direction and the speed.

- When he is calmly stepping over one pole in walk, put down two at a comfortable walk-stride distance for him.
- Get someone else to lead him and note where, say, his right fore takes off and lands – that is the length of his walk stride.
- You can, very gradually, build up to six poles in walk, letting him swing along with a free rein. This is also the beginning of slightly accentuating his gait, concentrating his mind more and introducing a long-and-low way of going because he is very likely, provided you give him a long rein, to lower his head and stretch out his neck to see where to put his feet.
- Think through how he must feel. If he does not have a long rein, he will be inhibited from lowering his head and may well go in a slightly or significantly hollowed outline – another feature of the flight-or-fight response (bad for mind and body in a schooling situation).
- If you don't rush this work, walk calmly but purposefully and, if necessary, tell him 'Head down', he will be fine. See also pages 78–79.

You can use the same process to start him trotting over poles but must be *most* careful not to push and frighten him. I would wait until Relaxation is very well established and habitual before trying canter poles, even one.

LATERAL SUPPLING/LOOSENING EXERCISES

Carefully progressed lateral work loosens, stretches and strengthens a horse and so makes all his work easier for him, helping to keep him relaxed. The key, as ever, is to progress slowly and properly.

EXERCISE 1 – TEACHING 'OVER'

Before you begin to ask your horse for turn about the forehand under saddle he needs to have an idea of what you want. A useful, in-hand preparation is being sure he moves over to both sides to light hand pressure on his side, where your leg will go (a little behind the girth) when you ask with it from the saddle. You can teach this in the stable from a young age as part of his stable manners. Do not push and lean on him as he will probably just push and lean back. Horses naturally yield to (move away from) intermittent pressure but they can lean into sustained pressure.

- *Initially, have a rope halter or ordinary headcollar and rope on him.*
- *Bring and keep his head a little towards you and low, with his poll about level with his withers, with your nearest hand. This will make him feel inclined towards moving his quarters away from you and the low head will help to maintain calmness.*
- *Depending on your horse, tap him lightly at least once per second on his side with your flat hand, the ends of your fingers or your thumb, or with a whip. He should move his body away from the irritation (like another horse nipping him). If a very light tap does not work fairly quickly, intensify the pressure until he does move.*
- *(Some trainers prefer to tap the hind leg to encourage the horse to move it away under him and in front of his other leg. This works well, but if he will respond to the other method he will already be used to feeling pressure in the right spot when mounted.)*

- *The instant you see a leg even just picking up, stop tapping so that the horse associates the move with the removal of the irritation.*
- *Stroke his neck, praise him and wait a few seconds before repeating.*
- *Do this to both sides, and in various places around the stable yard so that he will move his hindquarters over anywhere, when asked.*
- *Once the horse responds to the feel of your hand by moving across his leg on that side, teach him the command 'Over' by saying it as he starts to move his quarters, so that he associates the sound with the movement. Pretty soon, he will move to the lightest of touches and the command.*

Many horses will try to take the easy way out, in-hand or under saddle, and move the leg furthest from you sideways, then bring the leg nearest to you (on the same side as your hand aid) across to it, not crossing the legs. Although you have at least got a response in this early attempt, it is better to aim at getting him to cross the nearest leg over in front of the other one as soon as possible so that he makes a habit of the right response. With some horses, therefore, it will be more effective to tap the required leg with a schooling whip until he at least lifts it. When he does, stop tapping, wait a few seconds, stroking his neck, which is relaxing, and try again. The point of turns about the forehand is to get him crossing his hind legs, stretching his tissues, loosening up his joints and learning to move away from your leg pressure to give you control of the hindquarters. The last three do not happen if he does not actually cross his inside leg over.

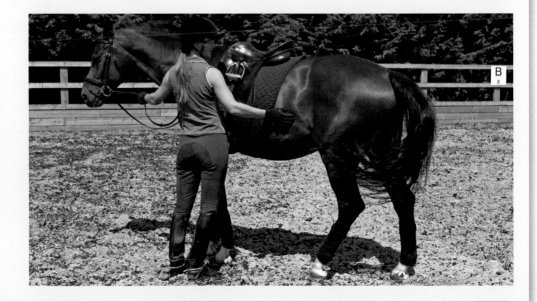

Mental rehearsal

With any new movement or exercise, it helps greatly if you rehearse it mentally and walk it out dismounted before you try it on your horse. This really does reduce the chances of your getting it wrong, confusing and upsetting your horse and finishing your session on a down note. Everything you and your horse do incorrectly confirms the wrong things in his mind, develops the wrong muscles and habits, and makes future progress harder. This does not mean that you need to be concerned about trying anything new without your teacher present, but that you should prepare yourself before trying it with your horse.

EXERCISE 2 – TURNS ABOUT THE FOREHAND

Before you attempt this work under saddle, your horse must be habitually calm and interested in his work, be willingly accepting the bit (see the Contact scale, page 84) and complying with your leg aids to go forward. In turn about the forehand, the horse makes a very small circle with his forefeet and moves his hindquarters around them. The horse needs to be flexed at the poll to the right for a turn that way (and vice versa), just so that you can see the corner of his right eye, no more. For now, be happy with just one step. Eventually, these turns can be quarter turns, half turns or even full turns, although full turns are not often required.

A good attempt at turn about the forehand to the left. The horse is relaxed in his mouth and correctly flexed to the left, crossing well with his left hind. The rider's left (asking) leg and heel could be down more and back from the hip rather than the knee, but she has achieved a good movement and a calm, compliant horse.

To ask for turn about the forehand under saddle to the right:

- *halt your horse softly, with him accepting and giving to a light contact and with his head in a natural position. It does not have to be a square halt in the early stages but a neat one*
- *flex his head to the right as described and position yourself with your right (inside) leg moved, from the hip, to behind the girth, and your left one dropping down passively, ready to control the quarters should the horse swing them too far and too fast*
- *your outside rein should be ready to check any tendency of the horse simply to walk forwards*
- *press or tap lightly and rhythmically with your right calf (do not raise your heel and dig it in) and say 'Over', assuming he complies with this.*
- *give the aid once or twice a second, increasing the pressure and maybe tapping behind your leg with a schooling whip if the horse does not comply. The very instant you get a response, stop pressing and praise him*
- *wait a few seconds, then try again*
- *walk around a little, then try to the left, and leave it there for now.*

If you are having problems, check that:

- *your preparation has been good*
- *you are positioning yourself properly*
- *you remain relaxed, straight and balanced yourself, and are not twisting your body in your keenness to get a result*
- *you are not transferring your keenness into your hands and giving unintentional, confusing rein signals, and that*
- *you are not actually blocking his movement by applying too much pressure with your outside leg as you anticipate that he might move his outside leg first.*

Walk around a little and try again. It often helps to look up and over to the right slightly, rather than down at your horse.

Once your horse is competent at turns about the forehand, do not keep practising them. Their purpose is to teach and check obedience to the leg, but they do put the horse's weight on his forehand so that he can lighten his quarters a little to move them. Almost always in your riding and schooling, you will want your horse to get used to taking his weight back on to his quarters to create lightness in the forehand, so performing turns about the forehand when they are not needed is counterproductive.

Walk pirouette is a more advanced movement which brings the horse's weight back on to his hindquarters, necessitating lift from the forehand and back. The movement also promotes suppleness and looseness and is part of the work of the Relaxation scale for more experienced horses.

EXERCISE 3 – LEG YIELD

This is the next suppling exercise to teach, once your horse is performing good turns about the forehand quite easily. In leg yield, the horse is flexed slightly away from the direction in which he is moving, and he moves sideways in a diagonal line towards a pre-determined point (see diagram), crossing his inside legs (on the side of the flexion) over in front of the outside ones. At first, it is easier for both of you to leg yield towards the manege fence, just a step or two at first, as horses naturally gravitate towards it, but eventually you can leg yield away from it, perform zig-zags and other movements.

The reason that the horse is flexed slightly away from the direction of movement is because this is easier for him, and this is a preliminary exercise suitable for novice horses. Flexing him the other way would constitute asking for half-pass, which is an advanced movement and more difficult because it demands weight back on the quarters and, because of the flexion, stretching the outside of the horse, and harder work for the outside legs (those on the side away from the flexion) which push the body over.

A very common error in leg yield is too much flexion in the head and neck, which encourages the horse to 'fall out' through his outside shoulder (in the direction of movement) and not actually cross his legs, simply making a diagonal line towards the fence. That can happen, though, even when the flexion is slight. You will have experienced sideways movement during turns about the forehand, so should be able to detect when the horse is not actually moving laterally and crossing his legs but simply making a straight, diagonal line towards the fence – his comfort zone.

The purposes of leg yield are to loosen the joints and tissues, to familiarize the horse with the feel of lateral movement of his whole body, to establish obedience to the leg and weight aids and to the rein aid of pressure against the side of the neck (just in front of the withers). The latter is an old, classical aid to which horses respond very readily by moving or keeping the forehand away from the pressure.

Try first in walk as this gives you both time to think about what you are doing.

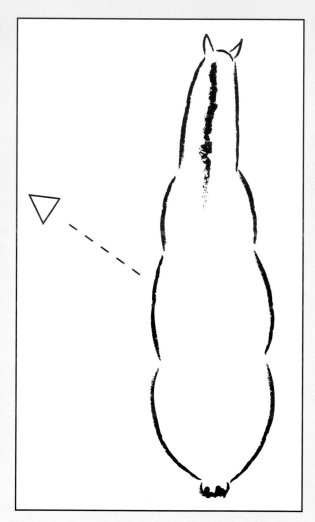

To ask for leg yield:

- walk on the right rein on the inside track (a metre in from the outside track), sitting centrally and balanced and with a comfortable, light contact that your horse is accepting
- slightly flex your horse at the poll to the right by gentle feels on the right rein, and bring your left rein to touch his neck just in front of the withers to prevent his shoulders leading too much and the horse just producing a straight line to the track, as many will
- now put some weight on to your outside seat bone by stepping down into your outside (left) stirrup (because where you put your weight your horse will go) and, with your inside (right) leg moved from the hip behind the girth, tap or squeeze once or twice per second, and ideally when his inside hind foot is lifting
- look over to the track. From the inside track, you should be there in a couple of strides, which is enough for now
- if you succeed, repeat on the left rein, leg yielding to the right.

Leg yield done down the fence gives the horse guidance as to his route and confirms obedience to the leg. It can be done with the head to the fence as well, which is more difficult for the horse. Leg yield does not ask for bend in the body and for only slight flexion of the head and neck away from the direction of movement. There is possibly rather a little too much flexion here.

If you are having problems:

- *either your in-hand preparation and your turns about the forehand have not been sufficiently absorbed or correctly carried out, or you are not making your aids clear and definite*
- *check your own position, relaxation and balance and try again with more inside leg (maybe supported by taps from your schooling whip in time with your leg aids) and more outside rein, sideways, to keep the shoulders in*
- *it won't happen on its own: you have to give definite, correct and clear aids, expect it to happen, look ahead and over to the track.*

Achieve leg yield on both reins for just a couple of steps first before asking for more. Too much, too soon can mentally and physically stress your horse, create bad associations and put him off. Eventually, you can travel from the quarter line to the track, from the track to the inside track, then later to the quarter line, from the centre line to the quarter line and vice versa. As with everything, do not rush your horse: let him get used to a few steps towards the fence first and progress gradually, keeping yourself relaxed, calm, straight and balanced.

Serpentines across the width of the school are a good exercise for developing suppleness and self-control. Here Sally and Clancy approach a corner of the school from the short side, which makes an easier start for Clancy as the track has guided him. He makes the turn after the corner with correct flexion and bend, and straightens up across the school, trotting towards the track on the next long side where he will turn left for another serpentine.

The concept of 'bend'

For many years most trainers and experienced riders have accepted the scientific evidence that the horse's spine in the back area has very little ability to bend laterally – so how can he bend round the rider's inside leg? The horse's ribcage plays a large part in this, as he can contract the muscles around and between his ribs in response to pressure from the rider's inside leg, bringing the ribs closer together, and can move his ribcage away from the leg, giving the illusion of spinal bend. The rider's outside leg is placed back from the hip to guard the hindquarters from moving out, so keeping the hind feet along their track.

The idea of bend seems to have been introduced partly because earlier trainers thought that the horse's spine was as flexible laterally as a human's spine, and because it is appealing, to our eyes, to have the horse's spine (as was thought) 'following the circumference of the circle or arc', as the phraseology usually goes.

The training benefit of suppleness and strength comes from the horse's need to stretch the tissues on the outside of his body and contract the muscles on the inside (speaking in relation to a circle or part-circle, every turn being part of a circle), and to move his outside limbs further than the inside ones. The inside hind leg in particular, takes more weight during the movement and is strengthened accordingly, providing of course that the horse is moving correctly.

MORE LATERAL MOVEMENTS

In shoulder fore, your horse will make four tracks very close together. You are just bringing his forehand in off the track by only one hoof's width, so that, seen from the front on, say, the left rein, you will see from the left, his right hind, right fore, left hind and left fore hooves (see diagram). That is all the displacement of the forehand to the left that you need.

In a 3-track shoulder-in, the angle of the body and the amount of bend is increased a little more, to about 30 degrees, so that our observer would see the right hind, right fore (obscuring the left hind) and the left fore hooves (see diagram). *In a more advanced shoulder-in*, the angle of the body may eventually be increased to 45 degrees, so that an observer would see the right hind, the left hind, the right fore and the left fore hooves, close together certainly, but clearly seen. This is called a 4-track shoulder-in. Some trainers say that this is too much to ask and others that the shoulder fore and 3-track shoulder-in are insufficient. Personally, I am usually content with the latter.

A good shoulder fore, all four feet being visible, if verging on a little too much bend in the neck.

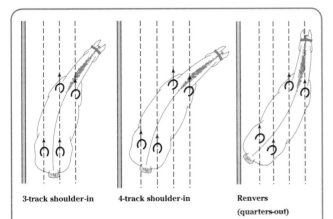

3-track shoulder-in   4-track shoulder-in   Renvers (quarters-out)

Renvers has been shown here to illustrate the difference between it and shoulder-in. In shoulder-in the horse looks *away* from the direction of travel; in *renvers* he looks *towards* it. *Renvers* is an advanced and more difficult movement.

As the horse progresses to a 4-track shoulder-in, the degree of bend around the rider's inside leg and the flexion of his head and neck increase slightly along with the angle to the side of the manege.

A common mistake, as with leg yield, is to get too much flexion in the head and neck (because it is easy to flex them) but little or no bend around the rider's inside leg. The horse's outside shoulder stays on the track and the result is a not performed movement!

Here the horse and rider are in a 4-track shoulder-in. Some trainers do use this movement but others feel that this amount of angle is no more beneficial than that required in the 3-track version.

EXERCISE 4A – SHOULDER FORE AND SHOULDER-IN

Shoulder fore is the forerunner to shoulder-in. Shoulder-in is traditionally regarded as the most important exercise in the trainer's repertoire for suppling, loosening-up, introducing the concept of the horse bending around the rider's inside leg, exerting control without 'getting heavy' (such as passing a scary object) and encouraging the horse to take more weight on his hindquarters as a first preparation for collection and more advanced movements. From the horse's viewpoint, shoulder fore is not difficult. All other lateral work is based on it and on shoulder-in, as well as the horse's grasping of a new concept of movement. Many horses go into it very easily if it is introduced subtly and for just a stride or two at first. This is where shoulder fore comes in.

In both shoulder fore and shoulder-in (and shoulder-out, see page 59), most trainers require the horse's hind feet to continue straight along his track without angling in but with the forefeet being carried slightly inwards so that he is bent, either more or less depending on the degree of the movement, around the slight pressure of the rider's inside leg. In this way the hind legs do not cross even though this is a lateral movement. Other trainers ask for more angulation inwards off the track (up to a 45-degree angle from the track) so that the horse's legs cross more or less depending on the degree of angle and bend asked for.

Shoulder fore is a gentle introduction, which the horse will not find difficult if his earlier schooling has been good and he is compliant, sound and not in pain or discomfort.

To ask for shoulder fore or shoulder-in left:
- *coming up to a corner (keep it shallow) in the manege, have your horse walking freely forward with a gentle bit contact and slight flexion at the poll (accepting the bit and your light contact, see the Contact scale, page 84)*
- *put yourself into 'position left': that is, your left seat bone and shoulder are slightly forward and your right leg slightly back from the hip, keeping his hind feet following his forefeet as you flex your horse's head and neck softly left and perform a 10m circle in the corner of the menage*
- *as you finish the circle and return to the track, stay slightly in position left as though you are going to continue the circle but as your horse's forehand just comes off the track again, keep the left flexion and bend but slightly alter your body position so that your right seat bone and shoulder are now forward pointing up the track (where you are also looking)*
- *slightly weight your right seat bone by stepping down a little into your right stirrup and your horse will follow your position and weight and, maintaining left bend and flexion, will travel up the track in shoulder fore or shoulder-in*

Emma and Thorney use the corner to create shoulder-in. Coming round the corner, pretend to continue the curve but instead continue straight on up the track. Only ask for as many strides as your horse is comfortable with.

- your rein aids will obviously help. Have a slightly open inside (left) rein: that is, carry it a little inwards away from his neck by moving your forearm and hand sideways (not down) to the left. Alternatively, you can create a more subtle effect by just turning your wrist over to the left so that your fingernails face the sky
- press your outside (right) rein against his neck on or in front of the withers in a gentle on-off pressure to help keep the forehand just off the track
- your inside (left) calf asks the horse to keep moving up the track by means of on-off nudges or squeezes just behind the girth. This also stimulates his inside hind to step more forward and deeply
- the school fence controls the hindquarters so, if necessary, you can use your right thigh to gently keep pushing the forehand in, in time with your outside rein aid.

If you are having problems:
- try again, intensifying the aids a little without any tension in your body or concern in your mind
- make sure that you are relaxed and correctly positioned. If you are not, your horse will be confused and will not know what to do. This raises his anxiety levels, which you do not want
- take your time and prepare by thinking and walking through it.

It is a good idea to have an observer at the far end of the track, who can tell you whether or not the hooves are positioned and visible as described above, confirming that you have managed it. Obviously, start with shoulder fore first and be happy with a couple of steps initially, then come out of it by circling left, not returning his forehand to the track, to keep up the bend round your left leg and maintain the flow and benefit of the exercise. It should result in a freer, more active walk. As your horse becomes familiar with and competent at shoulder fore, ask for more steps rather than for shoulder-in. When he can shoulder fore half-way up a long side, ask for a very few steps of a 3-track shoulder-in and eventually a 4-track shoulder-in, if you wish and your horse feels ready. Make sure your horse is comfortable with each step before progressing.

It is easier to start learning or schooling shoulder-in from a circle in a corner, as here, as the horse has support on two sides and is taken easily into the exercise. Later, he can build up to performing it in the open.

EXERCISE 4B – SHOULDER FORE AND -IN ON CIRCLES AND SPIRALS

Performing shoulder fore and -in on circles enhances the suppling effects of the exercise, but there is a change you need to be aware of.

- Put yourselves on a 20m circle, say to the right, and establish a comfortable, calm, active walk.
- Ask for shoulder fore or -in on the circle by asking for flexion of the poll and neck so that you can just see the corner of your horse's inside eye, put your right leg back from the hip to keep the hind feet on the circle's track and slightly weight your inside (right) seat bone to bring the forehand just in off the track.
- Use your outside rein as above, gently asking the head, neck and forehand to move in a little off the track.
- The reason for the change in which seat bone you weight is because – remember – where you put your weight your horse will go. If you weight your outside seat bone, he will drift outwards off the circle.

Always look ahead a good quarter of the way round your circle because horses almost always go where you look, as well, provided you do not prevent them with your body aids. You can carefully and very subtly spiral your horse down to smaller circles and out again (remember to change your weight aids and where you look when doing this) which is excellent for suppling, strengthening and subtle control of where you can put your horse, but you must be absolutely certain not to rush this work by asking firmly for a smaller circle than your horse is capable of.

He will tell you if he cannot manage it by resisting, coming out of bend, wiggling around, feeling unbalanced and stiff and so on, so the instant you feel any of this, or are having to work hard to maintain the position, you know you have asked too much of him for now. Go back to a very easy version of these exercises, and finish your session, however short, on a good note.

A little too much flexion at the poll and bend in the neck is a very common and easy mistake in shoulder-in, whether on a straight line or a circle. Both flexions should be slight, and the exercise performed mainly by means of the correct use of seat and legs.

EXERCISE 4C – SHOULDER-OUT OR COUNTER SHOULDER-IN

This exercise should be done once the horse understands shoulder-in. It has the same benefits as shoulder fore and -in but is more difficult for the horse as he is working with his head to the fence so does not have it to guide his body. It places the onus on you, too, to be very correct in your body position and aids because of this.

To ask for shoulder-out:
- *have your horse on, say, the right rein and, on reaching the end of a long side, perform a half circle to the right of no less than 8m and no more than 10m, on to the centre line in position right/right flexion and bend*
- *keeping position right and your slight flexion and bend, walk in a straight line towards the fence*
- *when your horse's head is almost over the outside track, keeping your slight right flexion, bring your outside (left) seat bone and shoulder slightly forward, pointing up the long side, weight your left seat bone a little and look up the track. Most horses familiar with these body position aids will now perform shoulder-out up the track*
- *to help him, use your intermittent pushing aid with your inside (right) leg, and keep his shoulders out towards the fence with your outside (left) rein, laid sideways on his neck in front of the withers.*
- *do place your outside (left) leg back from the hip against his side to stop his hindquarters swinging inwards and destroying both his bend and the benefits of the exercise.*

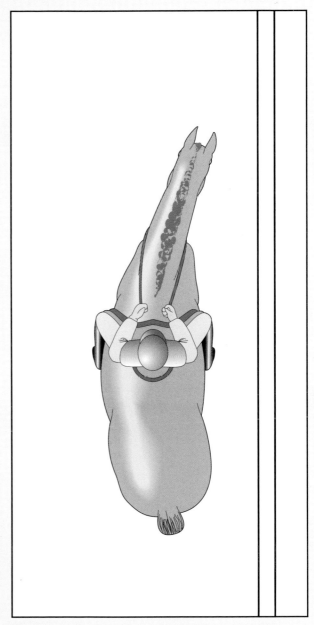

Shoulder-out is more difficult for the horse psychologically but has great training benefits. The onus is on the rider to come into and maintain the exercise correctly with clear and not forcible aids.

Shoulder-out on a circle can also be done once your horse is well used to this exercise on straight lines. The shoulders are, of course, out, off the circle track just slightly.

Imagine a circle to the right: put your horse into slight left flexion and bend, and weight your outside (right) seat bone; continue to look right around your circle.

With all these exercises – leg yield, shoulder fore, shoulder-in and shoulder-out – the major and most common fault is to demand too much flexion in the head and neck and – other than in leg yield, which does not ask for bend – no bend in the body. When done like this the exercises are just not performed, are useless and possibly damaging, and only serve to confuse and possibly upset the horse.

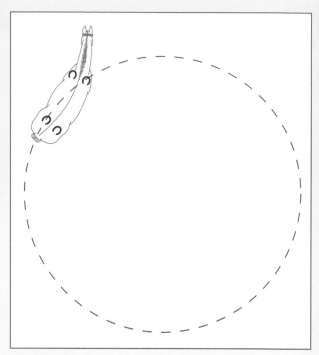

Shoulder-out on a circle

Another exercise that increases suppleness and is a little more difficult than shoulder-in or -out is travers. There is more detail on this in the Collection scale (see pages 135–137). In travers the horse is looking and bent in the direction of his movement, whereas in shoulder-in and -out he is flexed away from it. In travers, the horse travels with his forehand to the fence and his quarters carried in off the track. This means he has to push more with his outside hind leg, bringing it well under himself to do so.

Leg yield, shoulder fore, shoulder-in and shoulder-out are the only exercises the horse is asked to perform in which he is flexed away from the direction in which he is moving. The flexion is very slight and does not affect his view of where he is going.

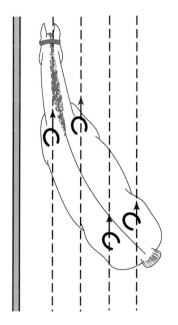

Travers (quarters-in)

TRANSITIONS

As the Relaxation scale is also about suppleness and looseness, and expanding the range of movement of the horse's joints and tissues, exercises that promote these qualities are included in this scale. Strengthening the horse's body – as well as stretching it with appropriate exercises – makes his work easier as it both develops him and reduces stiffness, which can inhibit him from working freely and willingly.

Transitions are a test of a horse's suppleness, balance and schooling, and they also develop and improve these qualities. The better these are, the more likely the horse is to halt square. In young horses, therefore, a decent halt with no legs trailing or much out of place is acceptable. Raising the head, poking the nose and resisting the bit are not acceptable, merely understandable if the rider pulls at the horse. In every case, the standard in transitions is for the horse to move smoothly from one gait to another (up or down) or to and from shortened and lengthened strides and therefore slower or faster tempos (speeds) within a gait. He should also to respond to half-halts without throwing up his head or resisting the rider's hand, assuming that the contact is fair and reasonable, not hard and rigid.

Transitions can be single, from one gait to the next above or below it (for example, trot to walk or trot to canter), or direct. Direct transitions omit one or sometimes more gaits (for example, walk to canter, halt to trot or canter to halt). Young, green, spoiled and unfit horses should be asked only for single transitions.

It would be difficult to perform a good transition to trot from a canter as forward-going as this.

EXERCISE 1 – HALF-HALT

The half-halt *is invaluable in transitions, and prepares and warns a horse that you are going to ask him for something different from what he is currently doing, as does saying his name softly.*

To use a half-halt:
- *simply apply your normal halt aid and release it as soon as your horse has responded by slowing down.*

The simplest halt aid:
- *first keep your seat still, lighten it a little and hug the horse gently with your thighs*
- *a split second later, keep your hands still, no longer moving with your horse's head.*

The different bit feel slightly restrains your horse and the still seat with gentle pressure of both thighs tells him that less 'forward movement' is required and makes it easier for him to engage his hindquarters to stop or slow down. This, in turn, results in an engaged slowing down or halt rather than the horse grinding gradually to a halt with his back down and his nose poked out and resisting the bit, as often happens when riders sit more heavily in the saddle and increase the bit pressure too much.

If you are having problems:
- *if the horse does not slow down at once, keep the aid on at the same strength and use your vocal command to slow, whatever you have chosen*
- *release the aid only the instant he slows down, either within the gait or to the gait below*
- *if you are still having a problem, ride a circle near the fence and, as you are approaching the fence on the curve (not directly facing it), apply your gentle but unmistakable slow/halt aid and say your command. The fence is a little inhibiting without actually blocking and maybe frightening him and will produce a slowing in his gait.*

If you want an upward transition, give a brief, gentle half-halt, release when he complies, then give your aid for the gait you want.

When schooling, do be prepared to use the voice sparingly (one simple word or phrase at a time, not a running conversation) to achieve your aims and help your horse. Remember to release the aid as soon as the horse takes up the new gait, and position your body accordingly to instruct him to maintain the gait until you ask for something different again.

This work strengthens your horse's back and hindquarter muscles, makes him adaptable within gaits and more easily able to use his body – in other words, it makes him stronger and looser.

EXERCISE 2 – REIN BACK

Rein back *is another technique that creates suppleness and strength, and so is included in the Relaxation/Suppleness/Looseness scale.*

The benefits of rein back in suppling work are to (carefully) work the joints and to engage the hindquarters and legs. It can be taught when the horse is capable of performing 15m circles in walk and trot easily, transitions from trot to canter and from canter to trot on 20m circles, and changes of rein through trot.

The horse moves each diagonal pair of legs (say, right fore and right hind, then left fore and left hind) back in a regular beat and actual stepping: that is, lifting the feet off the ground, moving them backwards and then landing them again, rather than the shuffle and slide sometimes seen in horses who do not fully accept the rider's aids, who are not ready for the exercise or who are confused by the rider's aids (because they are not clear, too harsh, or the rider is tense).

The rein back must be done straight: it is quite incorrect to allow crookedness and can be injurious to the horse. To control the hindquarters, use the leg on the side to which the horse is swinging a little more strongly than the other leg.

Some people do not teach rein back until the horse is pretty well established in his work and in the habit of complying with his rider's wishes. I prefer to have a manoeuvrable horse from early on, and teach a step or two back for the sake of convenience and safety. If you are at a crossroads while out hacking and your horse oversteps the line, it is good to be able to get him to move back rather than having to turn him round, which may not be possible depending on conditions.

Before teaching rein back, your horse should obey the command 'Back', taught on the ground as part of basic handling and stable manners. You can teach this by giving rhythmic little tugs, at least one per second, on the noseband of his headcollar, or by tapping his chest with a whip or fingertips, only stopping when he backs away to avoid the pressure. This is just what you want. As soon as he even lifts a foot to place it backwards, say 'Back' so that he will come to associate the movement with the command. One step is enough at first, then wait a few seconds and repeat. Soon, the word 'Back' will produce a backward step or two, then you can use the word from the saddle.

Initially, when riding, you might need an assistant to tap his chest as you give your aids (see the next page) and say 'Back'. The ground person must not give the command now. The horse will soon connect the two and the assistant can be dispensed with.

Anne and Lucy demonstrate good aids for a rein back. Anne has lightened her seat by leaning forward slightly from the hips, has a passively resisting contact on the reins to tell Lucy not to walk forward and is brushing backward with her legs. Lucy is reining back correctly, her legs moving in diagonal pairs.

To ask for rein back:

- come to an attentive halt, as square as possible without nagging the horse once he has stopped
- bring your upper body slightly forward to lighten your seat a little and, so, the horse's hindquarters
- keep a soft, restraining aid, with still hands, on the bit and brush your legs backwards against the horse's sides, saying 'Back' as you do so.
- the only active aid is your legs but your passive, restraining hands say 'Don't go forwards'
- if the horse does not move back, do not stop your aid but get your assistant to tap the horse's chest
- the instant he lifts a foot, completely stop all aids, vocal and physical. This tells him he can escape that particular pressure by moving backwards
- after several seconds, repeat, and be happy with just one step at first.

It is essential that the rider completely resists the temptation to pull the horse backwards with the hands, this is actually still taught in some quarters. The hands resist forward movement, that is all.

If you are having problems:

If the horse leans on the bit, throws up his head or pokes his nose, his response to the vocal command is not confirmed. He could also have a back or saddle problem or one with his mouth. It is more likely that he is not sure what to do.

In that case, gently give tiny, alternate feels on the bit to ask for yielding, ideally in time with the stepping of the hind feet if he is actually moving. This is, as described earlier, not at all the same as sawing his head down and pulling him back.

A horse who is becoming muscled up and supple should not show this reaction, it may be that he is not ready for the movement when ridden.

To stop the rein back:

- bring your upper body upright again
- release with your hands, then
- squeeze or tap with your legs, or just push a little with your seat bones if your horse will answer this aid, to ask for walk in the normal way.

It is inherent in traditional teaching that the horse should be made to walk forwards immediately at the end of the rein back to instil forward movement, but a horse who is truly forward and on the aids will be thinking forward and ready to go at any point. If you are out hacking and you back your horse for a safety reason such as waiting for traffic or to move away from people, you do not want him to have the habit of stepping forwards again as soon as you halt from the rein back as this could be dangerous.

Correct rein back involves each diagonal pair of legs moving back together, and alternately, as here. The rider has lightened her seat a little to make it easier for the horse, is resisting with her contact but not pulling back, and has brushed her legs backwards to ask for backward movement. This combination of aids is unique to rein back but it always helps to have your horse obedient to the vocal command 'back' and to use it as you give your physical aids.

EXERCISE 3 – COUNTER CANTER

The uses of counter canter are suppling (which is part of the Relaxation scale), strengthening and obedience. It is taught before flying changes of leg at the canter and is a preparatory exercise for it. Counter canter is taught when the horse is capable of performing a very few steps in rein back without resistance, moderate shortening and lengthening of stride in walk, trot and canter, good transitions up and down, canter circles of 15m with ease and in good balance, and performing walk-to-canter transitions. He needs a well-established and steady rhythm, to be able to flex and bend comfortably on circles and turns, and not to resist the bit or slow down on corners, turns and circles. He needs to give correct canter strike-offs on both leads, maintain them and not go disunited or break gait down to trot.

In counter canter, the horse canters on, say, the right rein but with the left fore leading and also slightly flexed and bent to the left. This presents little problem on a straight line but riders – and horses – can have problems when negotiating corners and building up to circles.

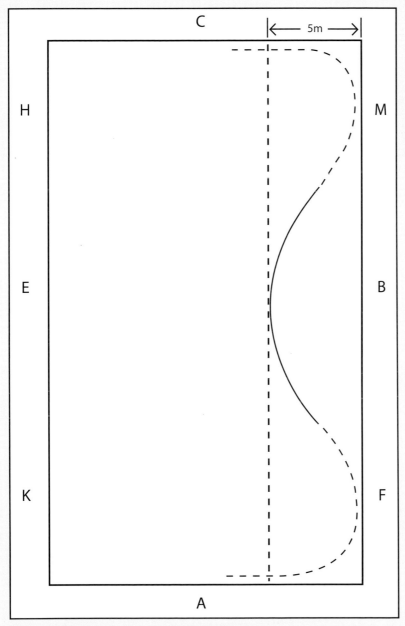

In left canter on the left rein, ride a shallow loop from F. The heavy line indicates the counter canter section.

To introduce counter canter – method one:

- *starting with a couple of strides only, canter round the school in a good working canter on the outside track and turn down on to the inside track of the next long side*
- *remember that, in canter, your inside seat bone and shoulder are forward very slightly: this is comfortable for the horse and instructs him to remain in canter on that leg*
- *keeping your slight inside flexion and bend, slightly weight your outside seat bone and stirrup and ask your horse to move over to the outside track by pressing with your inside thigh and calf, at the girth*
- *your inside rein, which is maintaining the flexion, can be pressed sideways on his neck to enhance the sideways feel to your aids*
- *depending on your horse, your outside hand can be carried a little away from his neck towards the school fence, until he reaches the track*
- *the instant he moves over, cease your inside leg and hand aids and say 'Good boy'*

- *as this is such a short distance, you should be there in about two strides*
- *release the weight from your outside seat bone and canter straight down the track*
- *give your horse a break on a free rein, then repeat on the other rein. That is enough for one day.*

Counter canter – method one

- *Canter, say, right, and ride half a 15m circle at F, touching the track on the short side just before A.*
- *On finishing the half circle, canter diagonally straight for the outside track between B and M.*
- *As your horse reaches the track and turns slightly to go on to it, maintain your right canter aids and he will give you a couple of strides of counter canter and stay in right canter on the track.*
- *Release your aids for right flexion and bend and bring your right seat bone and shoulder back level with their pairs and your horse will trot.*

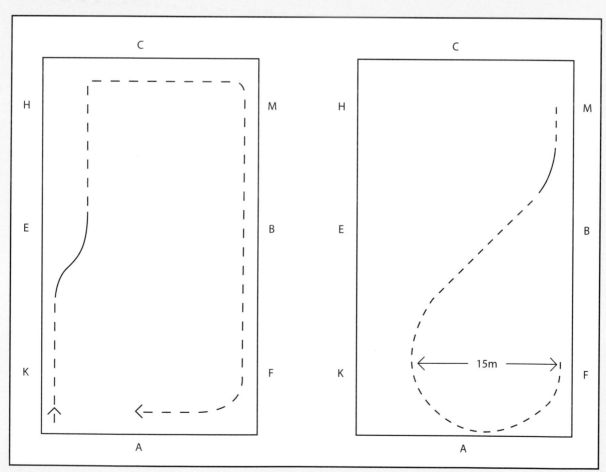

In both these diagrams, the solid line indicates the counter canter sections.

CHECKING THAT YOU HAVE ACQUIRED RELAXATION

Yourself: mentally, you need to feel confident, calm and be enjoying what you are doing. You must have no aching or excess tension anywhere in your body, although in order to control your movements you need tone in your muscles, which, in practice, means very slight muscular tension. If you find yourself riding crooked or with signs of tension, such as your head to one side, one shoulder, hand or hip higher than the other, tight buttock and leg muscles, collapsing at the waist and so on, or if someone you trust tells you you are doing these things, obviously you need to consciously tell yourself not to do them! There is a lot to be said for teaching yourself as you are going round and, above all, to give you and your horse *time* to absorb the movements you are attempting. Rushing a schooling session, a ride or a whole programme will just bring poor results, a hassled horse and a disappointed rider.

Your horse: the main signs of lack of relaxation in horses are rigidity, resistance, tension, tail thrashing, champing too much at the bit and an inability to do what you are asking. This can be caused by several things, mainly lack of understanding, discomfort or physical pain, or weakness. A relaxed horse who has not been rushed in his programme will be calm and content to comply with your requests, will perform easily the movements he has learnt to date (so showing that he is ready to move on) and he will perform them well and attentively.

HOW IT RELATES TO THE OTHER SCALES

Relaxation is the foundation scale and, in many people's view, the most important. Without it the horse's body is too tense to perform well and his mind is too geared towards defence and even survival to concentrate on his work and on learning. It is revisited every time you ride, from raw beginner to advanced horse, because Relaxation is always essential.

What a happy picture! Many people make the mistake of schooling in a manege or arena every day, which can be boring or unpleasant for a horse. It creates a more 'rounded' horse to take him out and about, with no pressure, just enjoying a relaxing hack. The long, loose rein used by this rider is fine in suitable areas out hacking and encourages the horse to walk out and maintain a ground-covering walk. It is never good to keep a horse on a firm or significant contact all the time – and it is always good to have some company!

Rhythm

The next scale is Rhythm. Many riders never give it a second thought, and even if they are familiar with the scales system they tend to regard it as of minor importance. In practice, a good, relentless rhythm makes the other scales easier somehow. Rhythm is not tempo: tempo means speed, and while most horses are sent on too fast, some go too slowly. Both faults make a good, reassuring rhythm impossible to attain.

WHAT IS IT?

Rhythm can be described as the regular beat of a horse's steps in any particular gait, like the drums in music. The strides should be unhesitating, even and level, neither rushed nor lazy. They should cover equal distances when on a straight line and last the same amount of time. Rhythm should remain constant for the gait in use on straight lines, around curves (turns, circles), in lateral work and through transitions within gaits. When a new gait is assumed, its natural rhythm must be taken up at once. The horse's work cannot be regarded as good if the rhythm is erratic or changes from movement to movement. If a movement results in loss of rhythm, it indicates that the training and/or riding are insufficient or faulty.

Anyone who is good at any aspect of music or at dancing will tell you that rhythm is an exhilaration you feel inside you, which carries or drives you on to the next note or step. If you lose your rhythm it ruins your, and your audience's, enjoyment of the music, not to mention that of your partner, if you are dancing in a pair – as you are when riding.

Regular rhythm promotes good balance in the horse, correct gaits and movements, and instils an inclination to move forward and on – all things we need for good equitation. Rhythm encourages a horse to swing along freely; this is especially important in a young horse who is still learning about free, forward movement. In more experienced horses, rhythm must be kept during the more advanced movements for them to be correct.

This five-year-old gelding, Comberton Clancy, has a rather tense nature and tends to be a little on edge, shown here by his demeanour and short gait in trot, and he is easily distracted. His rhythm, therefore, is not as regular as it could be. His rider, Sally, is exaggerating her rise in trot and using a strong rhythm to help him.

Trotting poles have many uses. Here Sally uses them to help Clancy find his trot rhythm, involving more deliberate use of his legs. He has realized that he has to measure his strides and trot purposefully to make it down the line without mishap, which produces a marked, strong rhythm as a by-product. Spirited horses sometimes rush poles, so the rider should move at the rhythm she wants and use the voice and outside rein to check the speed, backed up by tactful pressure from both legs to keep the hind end engaged so that the horse does not flatten.

The final result – Clancy swings along in a rhythmic, calm, energetic trot. His strides are noticeably longer, his tenseness has gone, his poll is the highest point of his outline and his face just in front of the vertical. Sally's contact throughout is light and tactful and Clancy works in self-balance. Brilliant!

THE RHYTHMS OF THE GAITS

Horses have their own rhythms, both as a species and as individuals, but they are more marked in some than in others. If a horse moves with an irregular rhythm when loose on good going, there is likely to be a problem of conformation, action or soundness.

There are four 'pure', natural rhythms – walk, trot, canter and gallop – but some breeds have a natural inclination for other gaits, such as the pace in which both legs on one side move at the same time in trot.

The walk is a 4-time gait, the trot 2-time, the canter 3-time and the gallop 4-time. Rein back is a 2-time gait.

A thought about the walk rhythm: most people understand that the horse must march along in a perfectly regular 1-2-3-4 beat, but some horses naturally have a short pause between 2 and 3, so go 1-2, 3-4. This is caused by the horse's natural conformation and, therefore, his action. If you try to make such horses conform to the perfectly regular 1-2-3-4 beat it can make life much harder for them, and it worries some. The 1-2, 3-4 rhythm is not hard to ride, and many riders do not notice it until they have it pointed out to them. I also find that it does not affect the horse's work from the viewpoint of impulsion, forwardness, correctness of gaits and movements, so I do not see the need to try to make the horse conform.

The 4-beat canter

Although pure, natural canter is certainly a 3-beat gait, some highly collected horses – and often those being overly restricted in the head and neck – show a 4-beat canter, with the footfalls in, say, right canter being: left hind, right hind, followed a split second later by the left fore (which ought to land with it) and then the right fore.

The view has been expressed that horses in high, true collection with very engaged hindquarters and legs simply cannot land the non-leading fore (which normally lands with the diagonal hind – right hind with left fore in right canter, for instance) at precisely the same moment as its diagonal hind partner, because they physically cannot get it down in time. Some classical trainers allow for this, but I agree with those who then lessen the amount of collection to allow the horse to produce a true, 3-beat gait, because the object of good riding is to enhance a horse's natural gaits under a rider.

As mentioned, the 4-beat canter also occurs in horses whose heads and necks are being held 'up and in' by the rider and in horses who are worked in very restrictive training equipment during groundwork. These horses, understandably, cannot move forward freely – in collection or any other state – and must be in pain a good deal of the time.

To repeat, it is faulty riding to hold the horse in or to think that we can support him on the bit. To display true, comfortable gaits, he needs only gentle, slight guidance from the bit (see Chapter 3, Contact) so that he can learn from very early days to work in self-balance and gradually 'come forward' and be 'through'. The state called 'throughness' is where the rider's aids pass through the horse's body from the hindquarters to the bit (or head if the horse is in a bitless bridle) and back again, the horse being truly 'on the aids' and working comfortably. Horses in this condition do not show 4-beat canters.

ASSESSING AND IMPROVING RHYTHM

Most horses have good natural rhythm but, understandably, lose it if they have difficulty balancing under a rider. This section gives you techniques for assessing your horse's rhythm plus effective ways of improving it.

YOUR HORSE

One of the best ways to get to know a horse's natural rhythm and action is to watch him moving confidently at liberty on an inviting surface, springy (not hard and shallow or deep and holding), *even* and, therefore, well-raked (not a rutted field), and with no nasty surprises such as holes, bricks, stones or blocks of wood, not to mention wire or horseshoes. It is noticeable that horses move differently in different schooling arenas depending on their surfaces.

Although it is possible for a horse to move rhythmically yet not be really swinging along in his gaits, rhythm is improved if the horse is comfortable and confident. In this case, his stride will nearly always lengthen and become more supple. A good way of testing this is to note whether or not he starts to overtrack in walk and track up in trot where he was not doing so previously. (Overtracking in walk means that the hind feet land in front of the fore prints on the same side. Tracking up in trot means that the hind feet land in the prints of the forefeet.) Horses who are not moving well, for any reason, barely track up in walk and often under-track in trot.

The important thing is not to chase the horse round so that he becomes excited but just to stimulate him to move gaily and naturally. Watch him carefully and try to absorb his rhythm in his different gaits for several minutes. If he is a jumper, he should be put over small to moderate fences, loose and wearing no equipment but leg protection, to see if he takes them within his rhythm and to gauge his ability to see his own stride, adjusting his stride and rhythm as he assesses his fence.

Watching a horse move at liberty on a good, even and comfortable surface in different gaits is the best way of discovering his natural rhythm.

Asking a horse to loose jump a moderately high fence is a good way of assessing his natural athleticism and his own eye for a stride. It also livens him up and encourages him to express his gaits and rhythm with more enthusiasm.

Once he is ridden, his rhythm should not change significantly under a good, sympathetic rider but may well do so under a stiff, hard or inexperienced one. Most young or unfit horses under saddle slow down (decrease tempo), because it is hard work carrying a rider when a horse is out of condition. This is especially true on turns, because they are harder work and more demanding of balance. It is one of the aims of correct development and schooling to have a horse maintain his regular rhythm in all his movements: this takes strength, balance and experience.

YOURSELF

Like your horse, you must be relaxed, correctly positioned in the saddle, very well balanced and, ideally, have a good, natural sense of rhythm. You must also be familiar with the footfalls of each gait.

- The walk is left hind, left fore, right hind, right fore.
- The trot is left hind with right fore, suspension, right hind with left fore, suspension.
- Left canter is right hind, left hind with right fore, left fore (leading), suspension.
- Right canter is left hind, right hind with left fore, right fore (leading), suspension.
- Left gallop is right hind, left hind, right fore, left fore (leading), suspension.
- Right gallop is left hind, right hind, left fore, right fore (leading), suspension.
- Rein back is right fore with left hind, left fore with right hind.

Loosen your seat and leg muscles, and let your legs and feet hang naturally downwards with no muscle use at all. Being able to do this enables you to properly feel your horse's back movements and natural rhythm.

Between most gaits, there is a clear 'changeover' or transition point. The exception is the point between canter and gallop. The difference between a fast canter and an actual gallop can be determined by the beat – is it 3-time or rapid 4-time? A good way to get the feel of your horse's rhythm is, starting in walk, to walk around with completely loose seat and leg muscles, no stirrups and a free rein, so that the horse can walk at his natural best. Hold your upper body erect, not stiff, and *still*, with your shoulders level so that there is no interference from your torso with your horse's movement. Absorb all the horse's movement from the waist downwards. Then, if it is safe to do so, close your eyes, centre yourself by

Establish a really relaxed, steady sitting trot with loose seat and legs, allowing your seat (but not your upper body) to swing along, dipping and rising with your horse's back movements. Interfere with him as little as possible and really feel his rhythm. Look where you are going – not down at his head, as this adversely affects your 'feel'.

Riding with your eyes closed for short distances (on the lunge, if you prefer, or led by a quiet helper) intensifies your sense of feel. Drop your awareness down into your centre, just below your navel and above your seat bones, and you could be amazed at what a different perspective this gives you of rhythm, movement and feel.

getting your awareness down into your seat and just feel the rhythm. Do not try to move your own seat in time with your horse's back movements, let his back movements move your seat. This can happen only if you are fully loose in your seat and legs. You should soon start to sense your horse's normal rhythm, or sense any irregularities in it.

If you have got the hang of this in walk, try the same in sitting trot. Be warned that any stiffness and banging about on your horse's back will wreck his rhythm and the scope of his stride, understandably. Therefore, stay loose, drop your legs down his sides (toes *not* kept up, which takes muscular effort and therefore creates a stiff lower leg) and absorb his movement by allowing the small of your back to hollow and flatten as your horse, respectively, lands and rises in suspension. This should make you aware of how easily his rhythm can be spoiled and his stride shortened by a stiff, thudding rider. When you mould to his movements his rhythm and stride improve.

Rider rhythm

It must be said that, like coordination and sensitivity, some people simply have little or no natural sense of rhythm and it is impossible to instil it. Rather than trying actively to create it, taking a relaxed, passive line and using help – such as adapting to your horse's rhythm or using a metronome when riding – can certainly help.

Those who have a good sense of rhythm usually not only like music but also really get into it and, almost subconsciously, tap their feet or fingers in perfect time to music, or sway to it. It is very noticeable that those who have little rhythmic feel do not do these things.

If you really like music, if you perform and play a musical instrument or sing, are good at dancing, have a good collection of music at home and enjoy going to performances and concerts, you almost certainly have a good sense of rhythm and will know it, anyway. Merely liking to have music playing most of the time does not necessarily indicate a good sense of rhythm.

PROBLEMS DUE TO LACK OF RHYTHM

As already mentioned, the Scales of Training are linked and interdependent. A horse who is not relaxed may go rhythmically but it will not be his natural rhythm; in such a horse the strides will be shorter, choppy and uneven. A good rider will always try to enhance a horse's natural rhythm rather than impose his own idea of rhythm on the horse. An arrhythmic gait will be erratic and cause differing stride lengths. This will adversely affect the horse's timing in all his movements and destroy the natural elasticity and flow of his gaits.

A horse who is not relaxed rarely goes in an ideal, regular rhythm. His body will be tense so he cannot flow with ease and power into his gait. Tense horses out of rhythm usually rush whatever they are doing, and produce shorter, choppy strides. On the other hand, a relaxed horse in rhythm, even a fairly green horse, enjoys moving and it encourages him to enjoy and concentrate on what his rider is asking.

Rhythm enhances Relaxation, and Relaxation enables Rhythm.

An example – canter pirouette

An advanced movement that often shows slowed, erratic rhythm and a laborious performance is canter pirouette. This is usually because:

- the horse has been asked for it before he is really ready (despite the fact that he may be competing at a level that requires it – this is no criterion as to his ability)
- the riding techniques being used to request it are inhibiting the horse's freedom to perform it
- he is simply not strong enough to sit on his hindquarters and hind legs and raise his back to bring his forehand round the turn
- riders often do not treat pirouette as a continuation of the canter but as a separate movement. You are still cantering but you are pirouetting as well.

This horse is clearly engaging his hindquarters well and performing only a small circle with his hind feet. However, from his facial expression he looks none too happy to me. I would like to see him working in front of the vertical on a lighter contact. The rider correctly has her outside leg back to prevent the quarters swinging left. It would help the horse if she carried her inside hand more to the inside and looked up and to the right, where she wants the horse to go.

REASONS FOR UNEVEN RHYTHM

Reasons for an uneven rhythm can be:
- tenseness, always caused by anxiety in the horse
- tenseness in the rider
- discomfort or pain as the horse tries to avoid it or lessen its effect
- worry about the actions of the rider
- being overly restricted in the head and neck
- concern, anxiety or excitement about something in his surroundings
- the ground surface, and
- the state of his feet.

There is also the issue of so-called 'bridle lameness' which is lameness that occurs due to compensatory movement caused by pain or discomfort in the mouth, which the horse is trying to avoid by holding himself awkwardly and moving in an altered way. This produces apparent lameness, but, upon investigation by a skilled person, who is usually sensitive and knowledgeable enough to spot the horse's facial expression and the signs of pain evidenced by a distorted and tense muzzle, it turns out to be nothing to do with the limbs or back but the mouth.

Mouth problems can be due to badly fitted or adjusted bits or bridles, a bit that is unsuitable in its action for the horse, harsh or insensitive use of the reins and bit, restrictive nosebands, restrictive martingales and training aids, dental problems and sores in the mouth or on the tongue.

The things to check in general are the mouth and teeth, the back, the condition and comfort of the feet, the saddle, girth and bridle and the quality of the riding techniques.

As always, the cause must be corrected before a relaxed rhythm will be produced.

When establishing a rhythm, sit calmly, give your horse his head and encourage him on without chasing him up, and just see what he gives you.

TECHNIQUES TO HELP FIND RHYTHM

If you are having a problem finding rhythm, remember what was said in Relaxation: you and your horse need to be relaxed. Sometimes, riders feel that they and their horse are truly relaxed when they are not. In the rider, too much tension (contracted muscles) in the seat and legs is a common problem, as is rigid, harsh and even pulling arms and hands. No horse can be relaxed ridden like this.

Get into the habit of dropping your weight down through your flexed ankles and heels – if you do not do this your knee and heel will keep rising, which means that you are tensing muscles in order to make this happen. Open your seat across your saddle, sit lightly on your two seat bones and drape your legs lightly down and round your horse's sides without pressure.

Give your horse a slightly longer rein than perhaps you think he needs and make absolutely certain that your hands and arms are in the correct position and *soft*. It is a *very* common and major mistake for riders to bring their horses into 'outline' more or less as soon as they get on and hold the head and neck 'in place' because they believe that the horse cannot balance without being 'supported'. This is completely wrong: to balance, in fact, horses need freedom of their heads and necks (commonly and correctly called their 'balancing poles'). Being ridden in this way actually tenses horses up, *prevents* the self-balance that is so important to humane, logical and light riding and stops the horse showing and using his natural rhythm.

Breathe deeply in time with your horse's breathing or, if you find this hard to tell, in time with his gait. In canter the horse's breathing is anyway tied in to his gait – he has to breathe out as his leading fore hits the ground and in during the moment of suspension, so you can easily manage this gait. To encourage your horse to swing on, give deep, outward sighs or breaths. To slow or stop him, take a sharp intake of breath.

Dressage to music
Dressage to recorded music is popular but, with the best efforts in the world, it often results in the rider unavoidably trying to match the horse's rhythm to the music instead of the music accompanying the horse. Displays and performances where the horse and rider have the advantage of live music following their every step is a world apart from working to recorded music.

Introduce your horse to poles by walking over a single pole first. Let him look at it, but keep a 'present' contact and expect him to walk over it.

Pole work, as described on page 48, effectively promotes good rhythm provided the poles are evenly spaced and set at a distance that is comfortable for the horse. Give him a long rein with a light contact and relaxed legs as you take him over the poles in walk, then trot and eventually canter. The ideal is for him to land exactly in the middle of the space between two poles, then there is less chance of his treading on them, which would ruin everything.

Music obviously has to come into this somewhere! Find tunes that fit with your horse's various gaits and either play them to yourself when riding or – even better – establish your gait/s and then sing the appropriate song as you ride along, either in your head or to your horse. Make sure your own seat and body movements match your horse's natural rhythm, then use the song to keep it regular. You could extend the music idea by singing to your horse as you work him loose. I used to own an old Thoroughbred mare who would go into a natural passage every time she heard music (probably from her days on racecourses and, later, as a show-jumper) but she was not fussy about its rhythm! Whatever music was played, she did a passage in her own rhythm.

Using your rise in trot is a very effective way of putting your horse into a regular rhythm – provided you have a good sense of rhythm yourself. Usually, I use and teach a minimalist rise – a forward-sit movement (described in my

2

Then take him over two poles with the same attitude.

3

In the approach, be positive and calm, have a light contact but let him know you're there, and firmly but gently, with your legs, ask him to trot on. Here the horse is in a good posture, approaching willingly and with interest.

4

Clancy's not too sure about this! He shows his concern but does not really object.

5

Getting used to it now. He swings along with confidence and enthusiasm, with Sally as tactful and encouraging as ever.

other books) rather than an up-down one, just skimming the seat of the saddle. However, using a more exaggerated rise, even to the point of taking your fork to the top of the pommel, and sitting deliberately but not heavily down again, really gets a horse swinging along in time with your seat. As soon as the rhythm is enlivened and regular, revert to a more normal rise.

Buy a small, portable metronome that clicks loudly, to wear round your neck. Set it carefully, after trial and error, to your horse's comfortable rhythm. This is most easily done by having a friend work him loose in all gaits so that you can set the rhythm and learn the three different settings for his natural rhythms in walk, trot and canter.

EXERCISES

EXERCISE 1 – KNOW YOUR HORSE'S RHYTHM

When getting to know a ridden horse's natural rhythm and tempo (speed, which is not the same as rhythm), it is important that he wears a saddle comfortable to him, as back discomfort will certainly distort his rhythm. He must also be allowed to move with a free head and neck, not on the lunge, under a relaxed, well-balanced and non-interfering rider who is just going along with him, on straight lines or very large circles, so that he will produce his natural beat in each gait. The rider needs to absorb these rhythms into her psyche so that they feel like the perfectly regular beats of a metronome.

Young horses will probably not have the balance to do this safely under even a good rider in trot and canter in a manege, so you will have to rely on loose schooling.

- *This method of familiarization is much easier without stirrups and with completely loose buttock and whole-leg muscles, as described earlier.*
- *Ask your horse simply to walk on and out and give him a free head and neck.*
- *If he slacks, give him a little tap with a schooling whip so that you do not have to use your legs, and say 'Walk on' brightly, to keep him going.*
- *Do this in trot and canter unless your horse is young or very green (I am assuming that you are capable of doing this!) but only if you are confident about it, as tension in you will affect his movement anyway.*

Giving your horse a free head and neck while riding without stirrups and keeping your seat and legs really loose is the best way of feeling his natural rhythm, and what he is doing with his hind legs.

EXERCISE 2 – MAKE THE RHYTHM

A rider can influence the horse's rhythm in any gait with the movements of her seat and legs. So, instead of following your horse's movements, you are asking him to follow yours.

- *Make sure that your seat is moving in the correct way for each gait in a faultless, regular rhythm, as this encourages the horse to follow your lead if he is unsure about anything.*
- *Be confident and definite about the rhythm so that the horse cannot possibly mistake it.*
- *Exaggerate your seat movement a little at first, so that he gets the message, but tone it down and return to minimal movements as soon as the rhythm has stabilized.*
- *To alter the tempo, if his rhythm is faulty, just slow down or speed up the movements of your seat, and your legs, if necessary, and use your voice in a calm or bright way, according to whether he needs to slow down or speed up – but you and he must maintain the all-important regular beat.*

Most trainers feel that rhythm is the bedrock of the gait, and speed is adjusted by the length of stride – a shortened stride to slow down and a lengthened one to speed up, but in the same metronomic rhythm.

Many people believe that they should impose their idea of a rhythm on their horse by driving him on forcefully into a fast, exaggerated gait while, at the same time, holding him in and up. In fact, finding the right rhythm is best done in a calm, unhurried but active gait in which the horse is clearly comfortable and happy to go forward.

Mature horses

If you have had your horse for some years you will probably know his history as regards injuries or other physical problems, such as diseases like navicular or osteoarthritis. Old injuries or degenerative diseases can result in permanent alterations in gait, which can affect a horse's action, striding and rhythm.

Old soft tissue injuries can adversely affect a horse's action and, therefore, his natural rhythm. The sorts of things that can cause trouble are:

- residual muscle 'knots'
- weakened tissue
- muscles that have not been routinely and carefully stretched
- chronic tendon and ligament injuries
- back injuries from badly fitting saddles or rugs
- injuries caused by working the horse incorrectly so that he has been forced into a bad and uncomfortable posture.

All these drawbacks can affect a horse psychologically, reducing his confidence to work freely because of stiffness or remaining pain.

Most horses naturally favour working to one side more than the other and may never have had any bodywork or correct schooling to even them up. If your horse is 'softer' to the right, for instance, his muscles on that side are possibly in permanent slight tension and shorter than those on his left side. When you take him to the left, he finds it difficult to stretch the tissues down the right side of his body to adopt the left bend and flexion you are asking for, and this may have been his *status quo* for years. The uneven rhythm this can produce may not be so noticeable on straight lines if you do not ask him to bend and flex to the inside, but if you do ask this of him, you may find that his gait becomes stilted, stiffer and less rhythmic, even giving the impression of lameness.

CHECKING THAT YOU HAVE ACQUIRED RHYTHM

A lovely example of an engaged horse on a light contact in medium trot. The only point that I would wish to amend would be the position of the horse's poll, which is not the highest point of her outline, although she is clearly not 'held in' or behind the vertical. If this were a moving picture, I am sure her rhythm would be regular and second nature to her.

Yourself: while working on this scale, you will have acquired a better sense of rhythm and action than you had before, so you should be aware of irregularities of beat. Probably the best way to check that you are working in a good rhythm is to play the tunes you have chosen as representing your horse's three gaits, or to sing them yourself to the beat of your metronome as you ride, and note whether or not you can keep to the rhythm naturally and are ready for and truly in time with the next beat, rather than having to consciously make an effort to match it.

As mentioned above, many people do not have a natural sense of rhythm or natural coordination, and if you really haven't, no one can give it to you. Using the techniques in this chapter will certainly help to improve matters, though.

Your horse: most horses have a natural sense of rhythm. When we become involved as riders, the major fault shown by most horses is that they start hurrying and shortening their steps. This is due to uncertainty and lack of relaxation. Some horses may become reluctant to go forward and they will slow down rather than rush.

If this description has fitted your horse in the past, you will be able to tell if the work you have been doing on Relaxation and Rhythm has had an effect on him (and you) because he will be far less inclined to either speed up and shorten or slow down and shorten. He will keep his swinging rhythm more often than not and be able to maintain it in his various gaits and movements, whatever standard he is at.

The more you work together in a relaxed, unpressured and forward way, the better your mutual rhythm will become.

HOW IT RELATES TO THE OTHER SCALES

Often, people cannot see how Rhythm affects the qualities of the other scales, but it has a strange ability to give a horse confidence. This in itself both relaxes and inspires horses (as it does many people when they are dancing) and makes it easier for a horse to do his work, so everything benefits. He can be seen to swing in his body and become enjoyably involved in his work rather than just putting up with it.

Many horses work to music with obvious enjoyment, even though it is something that is completely unknown in a wild horse's life.

Working without rhythm produces awkward, stilted paces and movements that can never produce anything of quality, as well as being unpleasant for both horse and rider. Achieving it makes life better all round.

A 4-beat canter: the left hind has just landed before its partner, the right fore. Technically faulty for canter, a 4-beat rhythm occurs in gallop (it is the natural rhythm for the gallop). This horse is clearly moving on a bit, and could be just about to go into gallop.

Contact

Poor contact probably causes more distress for horses than any other single factor in equitation. For the sake of our horses and in the name of humane, quality riding, we need to return to the old aim of schooling for self-carriage on the weight of the rein.

WHAT IS IT?

Contact is the nature and amount of the pressure that your horse feels on the bit in his mouth and that you feel via the reins in your hands. Riders and trainers should aim for the contact between their hands and their horse's mouth to be soft, elastic and ultimately as light as a feather, so that the rider can ride, according to the old and true maxim, on 'reins of silk'. The horse should be schooled to respond to the slightest change in contact created by the rider and, just as importantly, the rider needs to sense and react to the slightest change in contact created by the horse.

If a horse shows resistance the first thing the rider/trainer needs to think about is why it is happening, rather than assuming that the horse is being disobedient. The horse may be having some problem such as difficulty, discomfort, pain, confusion or anxiety, and his problems are very often presented and made obvious in his mouth but also in his way of going. A good rider *must* sense this and react accordingly, not necessarily by creating a firmer, reprimanding kind of contact and riding, but by wondering what is going wrong and being willing to find out with an open, educated mind.

During the early years of a horse's training, he should be schooled to respond to a light contact to ensure good control, but should require less direction from the rein and bit contact as he progresses.

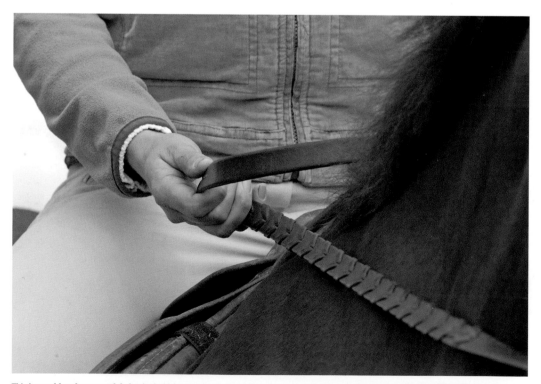

This is an old and very useful classical aid for turning to the inside. You can use it alone with your hand in place, like this, or in conjunction with an open inside rein (carrying the rein in to the centre of your circle or curve to invite the horse to turn). Simply turn your thumb outwards so that your fingernails face the sky and your horse will feel your aid even without any pressure on his mouth.

This is the effect when Sally, at my request, applies a stronger contact than Clancy is comfortable with. He is overbent, with his poll too low and his nose behind the vertical. He is on the forehand and out of balance and, as a result, his gait has become shortened as he backs off the contact. He looks really uncomfortable.

MISUNDERSTANDINGS ABOUT CONTACT

Over the last couple of decades, there has been a noticeable change in many people's attitude to contact. The result is that today we often see rigid and very firm contact applied as standard, with horses' heads and necks held firmly in the trainer's desired outline. However, this is the worst kind of contact because:

- it is physically very uncomfortable and even causes pain in the horse's mouth, head, neck and forehand
- it is confusing to the horse because he is being told to stop (bit pressure) at the same time as the rider's legs are telling him to go, and this confusion raises the horse's anxiety levels
- this technique causes the horse to hollow his back and disengage his hind legs – exactly the opposite of the correct, beneficial and safe posture.

Some trainers do seem to genuinely believe that it is necessary to hold the horse's head and neck in and up with a firm contact during groundwork or under saddle. This is supposed to 'support' him so that he can balance his body and also get him working in what is called a 'rounded' outline to develop the appropriate muscles, usually with the poll too low, the neck shortened and the muzzle drawn back towards the chest.

This posture of the head and neck is called 'hyperflexion' (also known as *Rollkur*) and is condemned by the Fédération Équestre Internationale (FEI), the body that governs many equestrian sports worldwide. The FEI announced in April 2008 that it condemns the practice as it is 'mentally abusive' and that it 'does not support it'.

The true situation is that the horse's head and neck are his balancing mechanism and he needs their freedom on a light contact so that he can balance himself and his rider. Training the horse to obey the voice, leg and seat aids, so that

A light but present contact that is 'in touch', without exerting too much physical or mental pressure on the horse. He is in a pleasant outline, his gait (in working trot) is regular, his poll is the highest point of his outline and his nose is slightly in front of the vertical.

his leg movements are under control, will enable the horse to come up increasingly to a light contact and develop his muscles without strain and potential injury. Given a light, comfortable contact in his mouth, the horse will not be afraid to accept it and its signals to work within a beneficial posture.

When the contact makes the horse go with his poll too low, so that the crest of his neck, a few vertebrae back from the poll, is the highest point (known as a 'broken neck' or 'broken crest' outline), and the line of his face from the side is behind, or even on, the vertical line, several disadvantages arise that riders and trainers need to be clear about:

- the horse's weight is inclined on to the forehand and forelegs, stressing them unreasonably
- this can cause the forelegs to land a little earlier than they should, which means that they are bearing more than their normal share of force. This has a braking, jarring effect on the legs and body, slowing down the horse and adversely affecting his forwardness and rhythm
- because of the way the horse's eyes are structured and how they work, the horse cannot see ahead of him, only down at the ground roughly where his feet land or just in front, depending on the degree of overbending or hyperflexion. This understandably causes anxiety, lack of confidence and even fear, all of which cause loss of calmness and relaxation.
- the horse's throat area is cramped so he cannot breathe freely, and he is unable to swallow the saliva produced by the stimulation of the bit in his mouth
- as the horse's balance system is sited within his ears, moving with the head in a constrained, unnatural position may well affect its functioning, resulting in feelings of dizziness and nausea.

The correct outline

The Fédération Équestre International's (FEI) own rules and all the most respected texts state that the correct outline is for the horse's poll to be the highest point of his outline, with his nose carried in front of an imaginary vertical line dropped from his forehead to the ground.

The only exception to the poll stipulation is in the case of mature stallions with developed crests, which are higher than the poll and *give the impression* that the poll is too low. If the stallion is 'going behind the vertical', this is still incorrect.

ASSESSING AND IMPROVING CONTACT

Try thinking of contact on a scale of 0 to 10, where 0 means no tension at all on the reins, and 10 is the strongest amount of contact you could exert. Then ask yourself what level of contact you and your horse normally have between you. You should be aiming, in a well-schooled, 'made' horse, at a contact of 0 to 1 – self-carriage on the weight of the rein. Even in a greener horse, if you have schooled him to voice, seat and leg aids as described so far in this book, and have a reliably steady, adhesive and loose seat, you should be getting habitual cooperation (unless terror and panic take over) and be riding with a contact of up to 3 on the scale.

Spoiled horses who have dull, insensitive, 'hard' mouths have become that way due to bad riding, firm and rigid contact, or badly timed pressure and release aids that have confused them. They may seem to need, and to take, a contact much firmer than 3 on the scale. However, reschooling them along the lines explained can result in a great improvement in the level of contact needed, and in their tendency to resist and lean on (push against) the bit. With spoiled horses, a change in the type of bit used also often helps.

There are several opinions as to why horses 'pull'. In fact, they are pushing against the bit. Those horses who have learned that if they can get the bit literally between their teeth (the premolars, which are the first cheek teeth in the horse's mouth) two things happen. First, the rider is helpless to stop them by means of the bit and, second, it prevents the pain caused by a harshly used bit because the teeth are not sensitive (if in good condition) and the horse himself is in control of the bit's movements.

The old saying 'it takes two to pull' is very true, and as a teacher and trainer I find that there are far more horses now than in the past who have 'hard' mouths. This is always due to consistently harsh use of the bit and much too firm a contact. The rider starts the pulling match and the horse has no option but either to join in or become badly overbent in his efforts to avoid the painful pressure, depending on his individual reaction. This type of contact can also trigger rearing, which is one of the most dangerous things a horse can do.

Reschooling, usually in a bit with a different action from the one the horse is used to, can work wonders if done by an empathetic, knowledgeable and skilled trainer, even in a horse with a permanently damaged mouth.

Even in fast gaits, a sensitively ridden, well-schooled horse should not need an excessively firm contact.

When thinking of contact, imagine three different types of handshake:

a tight, rigid handshake is very unpleasant and gives a domineering, uncaring message

a weak, floppy handshake does not inspire trust or strength of character

an in-between handshake – comfortable and reassuring – conveys a feeling of confidence and reliability.

Bitting and contact

Single-jointed snaffles are still very common but do not conform to the shape of a horse's mouth and, so, surely cannot be comfortable, even when lying quite still in the mouth. Snaffles with a lozenge or link in the middle of the mouthpiece must be much more comfortable. Some horses go calmly and well with eggbutt joints between the mouthpieces and the rings or cheeks of their bits, which give a fairly stable feel in the mouth, while others prefer the looser action of wire- or loose-ring bits.

Provided a rider has sensitive, steady hands with a sensitive, empathetic feel, I find that horses with 'problem' mouths (and minds) are often better in half-moon Pelham bits fitted just touching the corners of the mouth, creating *no* wrinkles, and with the curb chain well down in the curb/chin groove and adjusted so that it comes into effect only when the lower cheek of the bit is drawn back to an angle of 45 degrees with the line of the lips.

Bitting is a huge subject, and probably the most helpful thing is to try different bits until you find one that your horse clearly finds comfortable and which he listens to and complies with. There should be no excessive froth or saliva, no restless champing at the bit, no resistance and yawing and no tossing or twisting of the head.

All this assumes, of course, that the rider is not causing these behaviours with too hard or uneven a contact or with incomprehensible or unintentional movements and pressures on the bit. In other words, she needs to create a soft, elastic, sensitive and generally still and steady light contact. Any rigid, stiff, coercive contact in the middle or at the higher end of the suggested pressure scale is not humane or productive as far as the horse's comfort and cooperation are concerned, although there may be times when a firmer contact is necessary in fairly extreme situations, to get through to a horse for safety's sake.

A half-halt acts as a 'gathering together' and steadying aid, or as a warning that another aid is coming. Here Thorney is going 'flat' and not in a good posture or with acceptance of his bit.

After Emma's half-halt, he lifts himself, improves his posture and comes more into hand.

Conflicting messages

It is worth repeating that high bits and tight nosebands are very uncomfortable indeed and counterproductive to light and quick responses from the horse. In a horse's basic training, he is taught that a light pull on the reins means slow down or stop. If a bit is adjusted high in the mouth, the horse is experiencing a constant slow or stop aid even when the rider has no contact at all. The pressure of a high bit plus rider contact constitutes a very clear and firm slow down or stop instruction. How confusing for the horse, therefore, to be asked to go forward by the legs yet told by the bit contact to slow down!

Reasonable (logical and comfortable) fittings for bits

- A jointed mouthpiece should generally create no more than one wrinkle at the corners of the lips.
- A mouthpiece with no joints, such as a half-moon or ported Pelham or Kimblewick, should create a snug contact with the corners of the lips but not create wrinkles.
- The bridoon of a double bridle should fit like a jointed snaffle (one wrinkle).
- The curb bit of a double bridle should lie beneath the bridoon in the mouth and about 1cm or ½in lower than the bridoon, not touching the corners of the lips at all.
- A curb chain or strap should lie *in* the chin (or curb) groove, not above it, rubbing the jawbone.

A comfortable, well-fitting double bridle with an ordinary cavesson noseband. Despite the current fashion for using flash nosebands with curb bridles, a properly schooled horse does not need such a combination. If a horse needs his mouth kept shut he is not ready to wear any kind of curb bit. A double bridle should only be used by a very skilled rider on a horse who has been correctly brought on to accept and benefit from it.

'Seeking the contact'

This is a phrase that is instilled into most European-style riders the world over. The horse is supposed to want to reach forward to 'seek' the bit and want to make contact with it. We are also taught to school our horses to 'accept' the bit or contact.

However, modern research into equine behaviour and biomechanics shows that horses should, and can, be taught to go in self-balance from their earliest days, using the bit's signals as a source of instruction rather than actual support. It has been widely, although not exclusively, taught in European-style riding that a young horse needs a fairly firm, 'supportive' bit contact until he learns to balance himself under a rider, when a lighter contact is appropriate, but that he must still seek the contact.

If the horse is schooled as described earlier, to respond in-hand to the voice, to rope pressures on a halter or headcollar and, when ridden, to seat and leg aids, the hand and rein aids being all part of the aiding system, he will associate the aids throughout his life with light, quick responses and learn a light, responsive way of going that is comfortable for both him and his rider. He will have no cause to learn to 'lean' on the bit, to 'pull' (push against the bit), to go on his forehand which stresses his forelegs, or to develop a problem mouth.

A light, considerate contact with the horse swinging willingly along in good balance.

YOUR HORSE

Ask yourself first if your horse seems happy in his mouth. If he isn't, the contact from his point of view must be less than optimal. Signs of his not being happy are, as described earlier, a significantly unstable head position, excessive froth and saliva, resisting your contact or aids and, in some cases, stopping dead, running backwards and rearing. Causes include dental problems or poor use of the bit on your part. Finding a bit with which he is comfortable and which gives you a safe level of control (depending on the horse) has been discussed. Think about the following potential causes of discomfort and see what improvements you can make.

Nosebands

The next most common problem is *the tightness of his noseband*. Just like the idea of a horse needing to be 'supported' by having his head and neck held in place, another has grown along with it that the horse must have his mouth strapped tight shut, either to 'make him accept the bit' or to 'stabilize the position of the bit in his mouth', which will 'give him confidence that the bit is not going to bang against his teeth' or 'make your aids clearer to him because the bit will be held still'.

The horse's lower jaw is joined to his skull at a joint just below his ear (like ours) and, in order to be able to play gently with his bit *as is necessary in order for him to be comfortable with it and to 'accept' and use it*, the horse must, in fact, flex or open that joint very slightly so that he can have his mouth slightly open with a relaxed lower jaw. It is often taught that the horse's mouth must be closed to show that he accepts his bit, opening it noticeably being regarded as an evasion of the contact and very 'naughty'. If the horse is, indeed, unhappy with the contact we need to find out why, not simply prevent him telling us so. Having his mouth and lower jaw relaxed but more or less closed is very different from having it forcibly and tightly, even painfully, strapped shut.

The noseband, like the other straps on the horse's bridle, must be fitted so that you can easily slide a finger all round under all the straps including round the mouth, under the jaw and over the bridge of the nose.

A Grakle noseband, also known, for obvious reasons, as a figure-of-eight, is used on strong horses to discourage the horse from crossing his jaw to evade the bit and to prevent him opening his mouth. Although it needs to be fitted closely, it should permit a finger to be slid under it all around the head. The same remarks apply to it as for a flash noseband.

Flash nosebands are currently very popular. They are used, as are so many nosebands, to prevent the horse opening his mouth. With a horse who has developed the habit of opening his mouth too far they can be helpful in preventing this but, in order to achieve a horse happily mouthing his bit, comfortable with it (assuming it suits him) and able to 'give' to it correctly (which involves opening the mouth slightly), both the cavesson and flash straps must allow a finger to be slid easily under them all round the horse's head.

Teeth

Dental problems are an obvious cause of discomfort or pain in the mouth. Teeth wear and become sharp on the inner edges of the lower back teeth and the outer edges of the upper back teeth, cutting the cheeks and tongue: this commonly happens when a firm contact is taken, because the soft tissues are squashed between the bit mouthpiece, cheeks or rings and the teeth.

Hooks of unworn tooth can develop on the ends of the back lower molars and the ends of the front upper pre-molars. This is mainly due to not eating from ground level. When a horse drops his head to eat from the ground, his lower jaw moves forward very slightly so that the upper and lower back or cheek teeth are level with each other from front to back; eating with the head raised (as from a haynet) prevents this.

Grinding and biting surfaces can become uneven, teeth can become broken, lost or infected, and various other disorders can develop. Gum disease can make your horse's mouth tender, as can the teething process in youngsters. A veterinary surgeon or equine dental technician can put all these things right and should visit your horse, generally, twice a year – more often in young and old horses.

There is always the possibility that your horse has bad associations and memories of mouth pain from the past, and it can be very hard to overcome these except by ensuring as best you can that he does not have any pain or discomfort in your ownership.

Having gone through all the possible reasons why your horse is not comfortable in his mouth, you can take the necessary steps to put things right. Once a horse has grown accustomed to being comfortable, you will get a clearer picture of the contact he gives you. Does he have a fairly still head and mouth, with no fussing, champing or tossing? Does he respond to your bit aids as you wish or does he resist? And is he light in hand: that is, does he accept a light contact (remember the pressure scale mentioned earlier)? If he does all these things, contact from his end is good. If he does not, and you have worked through the problems listed in the rest of this section, the cause probably lies with the contact you are giving him.

Any discomfort in a horse's mouth can cause distraction, discomfort and anxiety. The front teeth though, in my experience, cause fewer problems than the back or cheek teeth.

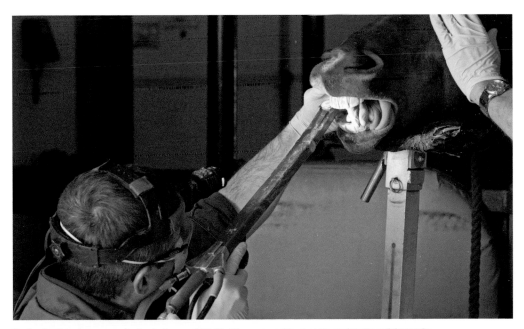

Equine dentistry is now a profession in its own right. Most horses accept treatment surprisingly well: just make sure that whoever treats your horse does so with knowledge, understanding and tact.

YOURSELF

It can be difficult to assess yourself, so ask a good teacher or knowledgeable friend their opinion of your hand contact. Ask them to watch you ride, observing what you do and, most importantly, what your horse does. A very common rider error, apart from applying too firm a contact, is busy hands. Riders' hands that move for no good reason, other than moving to go with the horse's head movements, or to give an aid, are a major source of confusion and irritation to horses.

A firm grip …

Covered hands

Another increasingly common fault is what are known as 'covered hands', where the wrists are flexed so that the fingernails face the rider's stomach. This creates a poor feel on the rein and a less sensitive contact, as does any hand or wrist position that breaks the classic straight line from elbow through hand to horse's mouth. An A-shape should be formed with your reins and forearms as your general, neutral position, the horse's mouth being the top of the A and your elbows the base.

… a more normal, moderate hold and …

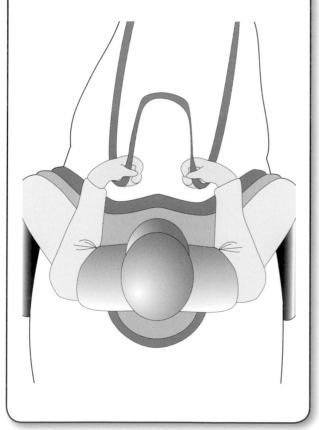

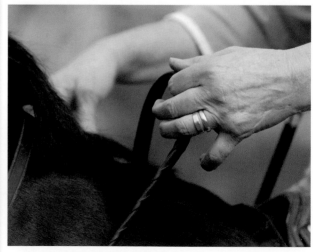

… a light, tactful hold. It is important to learn to 'play' your contact according to what your horse needs. Although today a firm grip and heavy contact is often taught, this is not conducive to skilled, diplomatic horsemanship and does not make for a happy, willingly compliant horse able to use his head, neck and body correctly.

The rider's hands, shoulders and elbows clearly betray tension and concern, if not anxiety, which always affects the contact and will certainly be felt by the horse in his mouth. Rigid, stiff hands and wrists, elbows held out away from the hips, and shoulders which are hunched and lifted all indicate lack of relaxation on the part of the rider.

Many riders, without realizing it, move their hands up and down with their bodies as they do rising trot. Another fault is to allow the shoulders to swing in time with the horse's rhythm, maybe not intentionally but because the rider feels loose, relaxed and that she is 'going with' her horse. As her shoulders move so, too, do her hands, swinging and swaying up and down and from side to side.

This method of holding the reins is useful to try for riders, including novices, who take too strong a hold on the reins and the horse's mouth, as it seems to make them less inclined to grip harshly.

My preferred method of holding double reins. The upper rein is attached to the highest bit in the horse's mouth (the bridoon of a double bridle or the bridoon ring of a Pelham) and the lower rein to the lowest bit (the curb of a double bridle or the curb ring of a Pelham). This is logical and makes it easier to use the two reins separately.

The more usual way of holding double reins: crossed, with the bridoon the lowest rein in the hand and the curb the highest.

It is difficult for us, as primates, to expect our hands to play a minor role in our riding, because we are so reliant on them in most aspects of our lives. The first step to improving your hands is, therefore, to learn to think of them as independent, like your seat, almost detached from your body or, at least, not associated with its movements. Whatever your body does, your hands must have a life of their own, and that life must be steady and minimalist in order not to worry your horse. Exercises to help you with all these faults are given in the following pages.

Keep in mind the pressure scale and always, always aim for the lightest contact that will give you a response. If a firmer contact is needed, get your response and revert to lightness as soon as you can. Eventually, if you time your aids correctly (applying them only when needed and stopping them the instant you get your response, so that your horse makes the right association), your horse will respond as required to the lightest possible contact.

The horse, having been taught to respond to bit pressures via the rein, cannot possibly know that, with some riders, not all bit pressures mean anything (just as some riders give leg pressures without meaning to or because they misunderstand how aids are perceived by the horse). This is a surefire way of creating a confused, dull, or conversely nervy, unresponsive horse. Move your hands or create a pressure on the bit, however light, only when you want to tell your horse something. Otherwise, keep them still, relaxed but not floppy or weak, and kind.

Less contact is generally far better than more, but no contact at all (the weight of the rein, in practice) is fine if the horse has been trained to work in a balanced posture, not on the forehand, with his back and belly up, as has already been explained.

What a lovely light contact, ideal flexion and bend! A happy horse and rider.

Less contact is generally better than more.

Hands free

We should all concentrate on riding mainly with our seats and legs rather than adopting a 'hands first' policy. The legs and sometimes the seat (the thighs being included in both) create the energy and direction, and the hands help to control the results and add the finishing touches. Riding mainly or entirely with the seat and legs is a necessary skill for herding or stock horses, leaving the rider's hands free for equipment, as it was for warhorses so that the rider had both hands free for weapons and fighting. However, horses ridden in this way are the result of careful, skilled schooling.

PROBLEMS DUE TO INAPPROPRIATE CONTACT

Horses who are never taught to respond correctly to the bit contact do not build up the rounded, muscularly developed physique that comes from gymnastic work. Those who are worked with a heavy, unyielding contact often try to compensate for the discomfort and pain in the mouth, neck and forehand by dropping their backs and trailing their hind legs. Consequently, they also do not develop a correct musculature for a strong, weight-carrying riding horse.

Horses who are kept on a contact more or less all the time they are being ridden, without being given breaks to stretch down and loosen up so that the blood can flow freely through the tissues to maintain them, become actually muscle bound and cumbersome, with little relaxation and poor balance. I am sure that they also suffer far more muscular strain and pain than their riders realize.

Horses who go 'behind the bit', that is who voluntarily go with their muzzles behind the vertical, hanging back from any bit contact, can be very difficult to correct. This is a serious fault, some horses learning to go this way as a means of avoiding almost any bit pressure. Very sensitive hands are needed to stay in passive contact with the horse going with his head in a good position, while using the legs to create energy and forward movement (not speed) in good balance.

If the horse puts his head down and in, make sure you are not causing it with your hands. Immediately raise your hands straight upwards for a few inches, with no backward direction at all, and give little, intermittent, upward feels on the bit, about two per second, to bring the head up to a better position. The instant this happens, return your hands to their normal place so that the horse associates his response with that particular action on your part, and praise him.

This habit of going behind the bit indicates a lack of forwardness, so it should be worked on. Even when the horse's mouth and the rider's hands are in order, this way of going can become a well-entrenched habit and can be very difficult to break.

A picture of equine misery. The excessive froth around the horse's mouth and his facial expression indicates his distress. The contact is too hard, the bridoon in particular appears too high and the coercive, compressed carriage of the head and neck is causing constriction in the throat area (hampering the horse's breathing and his ability to swallow his saliva) and forcing his muzzle behind the vertical (hampering his vision). The International Equestrian Federation has condemned this posture as mentally abusive and many experts feel that it also causes significant pain.

TECHNIQUES TO HELP FIND CONTACT

Always have in mind the pressure scale of contact and use the lightest contact that will get you a result.

As you ride, keep telling yourself to keep your elbows lightly in touch with your hips, with your upper arms dropped naturally downwards and held there with muscle tone. Holding your elbows out to the sides uses up energy needlessly and creates tension down your arms. Holding your elbows out in front of your hips can incline you to be

round shouldered and hunched and does spoil the sensitivity of your hands and also the quality of your contact.

If hands that do rising trot with you are your problem, as you rise (which should be more of a hips-forward movement than an upward one) think of pushing your hands slightly down, which will probably result in their staying in the right place.

Although this horse is on a fairly firm contact, which is causing him to assume a behind-the-vertical posture, very much worse examples are seen at all levels of riding and in all disciplines. In this type of restrictive head carriage, the horse cannot see clearly in front of him and the throat is cramped, hampering his breathing.

EXERCISES

EXERCISE 1 – ARMS AND SHOULDERS

- *Regularly exercise your shoulders and arms, mainly by making circles with your shoulders, raising them, pushing them back and then down.*
- *Do this several times just before you ride and finish the exercise with your shoulders pushed gently but definitely back and down, aiming to keep them there, without stiffness, all the time you ride.*

EXERCISE 2 – STILL HANDS

- *To keep your hands still, loop strong elastic bands through the front dees on your pommel and link your little fingers through them when you ride.*
- *Every time you feel a pull, you will know that you have moved your hands unnecessarily.*
- *Of course, you won't want to ride this way all the time, but as an exercise for a few minutes regularly, it can be a real reminder.*

EXERCISE 3 – USE A FRIEND!

- *Take a pair of reins and ask your friend to hold the hook-stud ends, or leave the bit attached for her to hold that, while you stand behind her and hold the buckle ends normally, as when riding or long-reining. Your friend is obviously the horse and you are the rider.*
- *Ask your friend to walk along and take your normal contact for, say, a medium walk. Ask your friend how it feels. Are her hands pulled backward? If she has to brace her arms to keep her hands forward, how difficult is this? Does she feel dominated? Does she feel that her forward movement is being restricted while at the same time you are telling her to walk on smartly? Are her arms aching and, if so, how long did it take before they began to do so?*
- *Next do the same for working trot. You will find that, at the run, the contact and its effects are exaggerated. If your contact is too firm, your friend might even tell you she can't possibly trot while you are pulling her back all the time.*
- *If you are both feeling energetic, go even faster for canter. Again, if your contact is too firm now your friend might even go on strike!*
- *Try different weights of contact to see which your friend finds easiest to work with (other than none at all). You'll probably find a gentle but present contact is her preferred choice.*
- *Next try pressing the outside rein against her arm and opening the inside one to see if she understands that you want a change of direction.*
- *Finally, change roles and repeat all this so that you, too, can experience how it feels to be restricted by someone else applying restriction and direction to your movements. It can be very enlightening – and sobering.*

YOUR HORSE

The standard way of checking your horse's contact is to perform 'give and take' with your reins. A horse trained correctly on a light contact and in self-balance more or less from the beginning, and one who is confident in his rider's hands will not be affected by this move and will retain his posture. The move is required in some dressage tests and is a useful one to do as a check at any time.

EXERCISE 4 – GIVE AND TAKE

- To perform it, some people just lift their hands up and forwards, then back again.
- Some make a D-shape by lifting their hands, then performing a half-circle towards the horse's head and back towards their stomach.
- Either way, the contact needs to be released and the horse is required to stay in posture, rhythm and tempo.

A more subtle way to give and take:
- always think of yourself as holding your reins between your thumb and index finger rather than with your whole fist

- then simply open the bottom three fingers of each hand and that will allow the rein forwards, giving your horse a few inches of rein
- close the fingers again to take it back, this serves the same purpose as 'give and take'.

This is an excellent, minimalist technique, which you can use at any time – other than in a dressage test when, despite the visibly loose rein, it might be marked as 'not performed' if the judge cannot see your fingers moving!

Giving the inside rein in canter. This is a test of self-carriage as, when this is done, so many horses then bend to the outside, showing lack of self-control of their bodies, even on a light outside rein contact. Of course, some riders actually train their horses to rely on rein contact for balance: this is not a good principle to follow and does not comply with the ideals of quality horsemanship.

CHECKING YOU HAVE ACQUIRED CONTACT

Use give and take as just described to check the stability of your horse's posture and way of going.

Be conscious of the feel you have in your (still) hands, which should be light, in touch and receiving gentle feedback from your horse. He should be going calmly with no untoward movement of his head and neck and no anxious fiddling with or champing of the bit. He needs to be giving you the feel of a quiet but 'listening' and moveable mouth. You must not feel that he is pulling at you, nor you at him, or that he is avoiding your contact.

Trot is a good gait for assessing contact. If he is moving his head in time with his gait in trot (a gait in which the head should be practically still), nodding it or flexing it from side to side as he goes, he is almost certainly doing this in response to too strong a contact. No horse trots like that when free and not ridden. This is quite a common fault. Lighten up the contact, usually by lengthening the reins a little and/or relaxing your hands and wrists. Remember, your horse must not be held in on a contact strong enough to cause unwarranted head movements and/or a shortened neck or, conversely, a rigidly still head and neck.

HOW IT RELATES TO THE OTHER SCALES

A poor contact adversely affects your horse's work throughout all the scales of training. It destroys Relaxation if it is too firm, erratic and demanding; it prevents Rhythm from swinging along, again if it is too firm or if your hands are not still, and works directly against the horse's finding his own balance under weight. It can make Straightness a chore to achieve if the horse is swinging his body around, even slightly, to relieve the discomfort in his mouth and forehand; it can certainly inhibit forwardness and, therefore, engagement and Impulsion, necessitating very strong driving aids from the rider's legs; and if all this preceding work is not up to standard, true, quality Collection will never be achieved because it depends on self-carriage and lightness.

Too little contact is a far less serious scenario but most horses do need an initial encouragement to work up to and flex to a light contact in order to achieve the necessary gymnastic posture of back and belly up, hindquarters tucked under in engagement and the head and neck stretching in an arc forward and down, or up depending on his level, but not in hyperflexion.

Straightness

Many riders do not understand the importance of straightness. It is essential for achieving good quality gaits and movements and there are several useful techniques for acquiring it. A horse and rider both must be fairly reliably straight before going on to develop impulsion.

WHAT IS IT?

Straightness describes a horse whose forehand is in line with his hindquarters and whose hind feet follow along the same track as the forefeet. His head should be directly in front of his shoulders on straight lines and should look round the bend of a curved track. All this applies unless he is asked for a contrary bend or flexion. Most people now accept the scientifically proved fact that it is anatomically impossible for the horse's spine to bend sufficiently to follow a curved track. Watching any reasonably well-schooled horse, however, will show that his hind feet can follow his forefeet along a curve. How the horse achieves this is explained on page 102. When he is straight, his weight and that of his

rider is evenly distributed throughout the two halves of his body. This feels right to both horse and rider and makes movement easier. The horse's hind legs can do a good job of propulsion, sending his impulsive force and energy evenly and correctly forward through his spine and other joints to his mouth. Here, a gentle, restraining feel on the bit encourages the horse to work in a good posture and at the speed we want, although speed can be controlled with the seat and legs as well. These benefits of straightness make for controllability and physical development, suppling and strengthening the horse evenly with the aim of making him a calm, comfortable and responsive ride.

An ideal example of a horse with perfectly straight action.

Like people, horses are born favouring one side of their bodies more than the other – they are naturally crooked. Just as most people are right handed, for example, most horses seem to work better on the left rein than the right. Many reasons have been put forward for this natural crookedness. Some maintain that this tendency originates in the brain, others that it has a genetic basis, or that it depends on which side the foal mostly lay in the womb, or, when it comes to preferring the left side, on the fact that many people still follow the old practice of always leading horses from the left. There are various other theories.

The side to which the horse works best is usually called his 'soft' side and the other his 'stiff' side. The muscles on his soft side, it seems, are very slightly more contracted, in tension, than those on his stiff side, so when we ask him to flex and 'bend' to his stiff side, let's say his right, he finds it physically more difficult to stretch the muscles and tissues on his left side.

An obvious question is, 'if he is naturally slightly crooked, surely that is how he is most comfortable, and he has been used to it from birth, so why do we have to straighten him?' The answer is given above – to direct the energetic forces

evenly through his body so that he can carry our weight; to work more gymnastically than he would if he were not ridden, without increasing the likelihood of his experiencing uneven stress and strain, and of sustaining injuries as a result. A straight horse is more comfortable for us to ride and, in a work situation, it must surely be more comfortable and easier for the horse to work with a straight body.

A straight horse presents us with fewer resistances than a crooked one because his body is more comfortable. All else being equal, he does not associate being ridden with the discomfort of working in a crooked state or with a rider who is being thrown into a poor position as she tries to compensate for her horse's crookedness.

When a horse is straight it is also much easier to make him 'through', because the energy he offers his rider, and the controlling and directing aids she gives to make use of it, operate with no diversions or blocks in his body due to crookedness. The horse will stay sounder because no part of his body is receiving more force or weight than it should and, from the point of view of being a riding horse, he is moving correctly and with greater ease and comfort than a crooked horse.

Straight rider, crooked horse. The head and neck are bent slightly to the left but the horse is wandering to the right.

The rider has let her weight slip very slightly right and, therefore, the horse is starting to move right.

ASSESSING AND IMPROVING STRAIGHTNESS

How can you assess straightness in your horse and yourself? The use of mirrors in a school or guidance from a helpful friend will assist you with this.

YOUR HORSE

A simple way to assess straightness is to ride towards your reflection in a mirror, if you can find a school that has mirrors. Otherwise, ask your teacher or a reliable friend to let you know whether or not your horse is moving straight towards them. Do this going away, as well. Trot is the easiest gait in which your horse can achieve straightness, then canter, then walk: it is quite difficult to walk a straight, non-wobbly line.

Ask your observer also to watch him on curved tracks in all three gaits, but be careful of the canter in young, green or unfit horses, as even a 20m circle can be difficult and unbalancing for them.

If you keep your seat and thigh muscles relaxed they are more likely to be sensitive to your horse's motion and position, and you may well be able to feel whether or not he is straight. This is an important skill to cultivate. When you get the feedback from your observer, note what you are feeling so that you can recognize it in future and correct the situation, if necessary.

How your horse does it

Your horse achieves straightness on curved tracks when asked for bend and flexion by his rider by contracting the muscles on his inside side, such as his back muscles, those along his belly and between his ribs. This pushes his ribcage and belly out a little, which makes room for his inside hind stifle to come forward on the curve without being slightly obstructed by his belly. In this way, his hind feet follow his forefeet round the curve. If you get a chance to watch a horse at liberty performing a turn or noticeable curve, you will see that he prefers to turn on his centre without bend or flexion as this is easier: at least his hind feet will swing out a little, depending on the curve. When he is ridden, we aim to prevent this by putting our outside leg back from the hip to keep the hind feet on the curve, which is harder work for the horse.

A friend of mine took the door off an old wardrobe as it had a long dressing mirror on the front, and fixed it up at the end of her school, where it did good service for a while. She took it down because she often found dead birds at its base, who had flown into it and broken their necks.

Sally and Clancy in a perfectly straight canter.

YOURSELF

First of all, check the simple things like ensuring that your saddle is evenly placed on your horse's back and that your stirrups are level. Before mounting, do some sideways stretching exercises, leg swings, ankle circles, shoulder circles and head circles.

Again, try to use mirrors, if possible, but otherwise ask your teacher or friend. If you have mastered Relaxation and Rhythm for yourself you should have no major problems such as collapsing at the waist or hip, riding with your hands often at different levels, one shoulder higher than the other or your head tilted to one side or poking forward. These are all signs of tension and will prevent you achieving straightness.

The corridor of the aids

This is an old classical concept that really helps you and your horse to stay straight on straight lines and curved ones.

Just imagine that you are riding down a narrow corridor on the track you want, the walls being formed by your reins and legs on each side. If you allow your horse to deviate, you will bump into the walls. Be sure to stay relaxed as tensing up will actually make it more difficult. If you stay calm and keep the image in your mind you will find that it really works.

Riding towards a traffic cone or some other marker is useful for concentrating your aim.

Pretend that you are riding down a narrow corridor and mustn't touch the walls.

PROBLEMS ARISING FROM LACK OF STRAIGHTNESS

Anyone who has ridden a significantly crooked horse knows how uncomfortable it is. The rider is often placed in a twisted position and feels stresses and forces in her body in an uneven way, and may well end up with backache. Crooked horses do not accept or respond to the aids as smoothly or easily as straight ones and have no concept of straightness or crookedness; they merely know that they are uncomfortable or are being asked to do something they cannot cope with.

As explained in the section on Preparation, the reason many trainers place Straightness before Impulsion in the Scales of Training is because it is counterproductive to have a horse go with impulsion if all that force and energy created by engaged hindquarters is being blocked by a crooked body or being unevenly distributed through it. Working with impulsion within a crooked framework will cause uneven development of muscles and can cause undue stress to some parts of the body at the expense of others, whether bones, joints or soft tissues. Also, it is more difficult for a crooked horse to be balanced and to develop impulsion.

There is also the effect on his mind. If the rider ploughs on with demanding, athletic work such as obtaining Impulsion without first acquiring pretty good Straightness, the horse will find it more difficult and may come to associate work with discomfort, unpleasantness or even pain.

To check from a side view whether or not a horse is straight just see where his feet land. His hind feet should land on the same line or track as his forefeet, as here.

TECHNIQUES TO HELP FIND STRAIGHTNESS

The conformation for the job

Horses bred specifically for sprint racing – for instance, some Thoroughbred sprinters – are often rather croup high, with long hind legs and short backs. To avoid hitting their forelegs and feet, some of them move in a sort of rhumba motion with their hindquarters, their hind legs wide and their hind feet falling to the side and well ahead of the fore prints. This conformation is the opposite to that required for dressage horses, many of whom are desired to be 'uphill'.

The interesting difference is that the dressage horses are intentionally bred that way whereas, in the sprinting Thoroughbreds, the croup-high/long hind legs feature has developed on its own because of the demand in the industry for blistering speed – natural selection in action in domesticity. This trend started in America but is now found throughout the world where Thoroughbreds are raced.

A naturally square stance with a leg at each corner. Very attractive.

May I start this section with a technique that you should *not* use? We sometimes read or hear that because a horse's hips are wider than his shoulders, his hind feet are set further apart than his forefeet. Therefore, they do not travel or land on exactly the same track as the forefeet. In a fenced school, it is said, this means that when a horse is working next to the fence and, as horses do, gravitating towards it or hugging it a bit (psychologically 'leaning' on it), he will go with his outside shoulder and hip right next to it. His outside hind and forefeet will travel on the same track but, because of the difference in width of his shoulders and hips and the way he is positioning himself, his inside fore will land further out than his inside hind, so he is actually travelling slightly crookedly on three close tracks. To correct this, it is advised that the rider brings the horse's shoulders fractionally in off the track whenever she is riding on a straight line next to the fence, so that the feet are more aligned – but still, presumably, not landing in the same plane because of the width discrepancy.

None of this is true or applicable. Take any normal, well-conformed riding horse with good action, stand him in a square halt and look at him from a little way behind, with his tail knotted up or someone holding it well out of the way. Study how his hind legs stand and you will note that his hind legs and feet more or less exactly obscure his forelegs and feet. His hind feet do not, in fact, stand wider apart than his forefeet. The reason for this is that the horse's upper hind legs are angled slightly inwards down towards the hocks; from there, the cannons drop down straight behind the front cannons. This means that the hind legs and feet *do* follow in the same plane as the fore ones, and land on the same tracks. Carefully watch the horse from the back as he is walked and trotted up with a *loose* lead rope and you can confirm that his hind feet are in line with his fore feet. Do this on some fresh ground, such as a smooth beach when the tide has recently gone out, or on some freshly raked bare earth or a newly harrowed manege, and you can check that the hind hooves do not land to the outside of the fore ones but on exactly the same line, unless the horse 'goes wide behind', which is a recognized defect.

There is no need, therefore, to bring your horse's shoulders in off the track to straighten him up: if you do you will be making him crooked and uncomfortable, and thus increasing his difficulties.

> Don't believe everything you read! Check it and try it out in practice. A lot of human logic applied to horses is just not accurate.

YOUR HORSE

When you want to straighten your horse, do not take the easy way out and put your leg back to move his quarters into line with his shoulders, as this inevitably puts his weight more on to his forehand, which, of course, we do not want. Instead, bring the shoulders in front of the quarters by pushing them over with the relevant rein. Then, if necessary, bring the whole horse back on to your required track.

Just a light tap or press with the knuckles on the side of the withers will move the horse's forehand over to straighten him.

Never use the inside rein to pull the forehand round, as you will probably only succeed in turning the head and neck. Instead, use the pushing outside rein aid (intermittent pushes with the rein laid sideways on the neck) which turns the whole forehand. This is instantly understood by horses and retains their balance. You can also just lightly tap the outside of the withers with your knuckles or even just the tip of one finger. One tap of this little aid is often enough.

Use your outside rein to turn the forehand rather than pulling on the inside one – a crude aid not popular with horses and which often turns the head and neck but not the shoulders. Here, the outside rein in pressing lightly against the horse's neck whilst the inside one is being carried slightly inwards, inviting the horse to turn.

Remember that where you put your weight, and where you look, your horse will go.

YOURSELF

Being able to 'be in the moment' and concentrate on what you are doing at any one time is a huge bonus. Try to drop your awareness down into your 'centre', just below your tummy button and hovering above your seat bones, and ride from there with your seat. This visualization really works if you allow yourself to do it properly, with relaxation.

Keep your elbows skimming your hips all the time and, if your fault is turned-out toes, try to turn them in but *don't* force them as this will cause stiffness and discomfort. The idea of this is to neaten your position and close your legs gently into your horse without pressure.

Some trainers stipulate that, in straightness, the rider must have an even feel on both reins, but others, who work on the principle that the outside rein is the so-called 'master rein' that controls the horse's speed, prefer a gentle, consistent contact on the outside rein and a lesser or more intermittent one on the inside rein, which does most of the communicating. Once the horse is able to function well on the lightest of contacts this becomes almost irrelevant but, otherwise, it has a lot going for it. Horses do seem to work more freely when they do *not* have a contact that is equal in both weight (pressure) and nature on both reins, almost as though they do not feel so 'hemmed in' – which is understandable for a flight animal. If sensitively applied, this by no means actually makes them crooked, as may reasonably be suspected, and the difference is slight, anyway.

Think of your seat bones as two wheels of a vehicle travelling down a railway track, visualizing the track beneath you as you ride. Just put the wheels on the track and go. Remember that, generally, your shoulders should be above your hips so that you are not riding with a twisted upper body. Remember also the position for canter – inside seat bone and shoulder forward a little on the side of the leading leg. Riding with your inside seat bone forward and your outside shoulder forward twists your upper body, and is incorrect, although it is commonly taught.

Get a friend to watch you as you ride and ask them to indicate if you are not sitting straight in the saddle.

If your horse is drifting off line, perhaps it is your fault. Straighten up your seat bones and weight them evenly, and see if things improve. If it is not your fault, slightly weight the seat bone on the side away from that to which your horse is drifting and he will come back under you, particularly if you apply your outside rein and leg as well (those away from the direction in which you want him to go). For instance, if your horse is drifting to the right, slightly weight your left seat bone and stirrup and give intermittent pushes with your right rein and leg.

Make a habit of looking where you want to go. I would say that a good 90 per cent of riders look down at their horses when they ride. Believe it or not, horses can find this oppressive and inhibiting. It also takes your concentration away from the technique of riding with your seat. To prove this, try riding around with your eyes closed and see where your concentration ends up – in your centre/seat area because that is your main contact with your horse. Many problems of potato-shaped circles could be solved if riders would look about a quarter of the way round their circle, keeping their eyes this far ahead of their horse's actual position on the circle track. Just before you come out of the circle, look towards the next marker or ahead down whatever track you have chosen. Do try it because it really works well.

If it seems that you have chronic problems that are affecting your own straightness, seriously consider going to classes in yoga, Pilates and Alexander Technique, also Feldenkrais technique. These are really useful for strengthening, stretching and evening up the two sides of your body, which is bound to improve your seat and position when riding.

Most local authorities run classes for these modalities, so a phone call should come up with venues and times. Also, notices are often posted in local libraries and sports centres. With a new pursuit of this type, it is probably safer to start off with a qualified instructor and a bit of moral support from other students, then you can carry on on your own later. Of course, there is always the internet for further information.

EXERCISES

EXERCISE 1 – STRETCHING THE STIFF SIDE

If your horse, like most, has a soft and a stiff side, try bodywork from the ground to even him up. It is well worth having a specialist such as an equine sports massage therapist come to discuss what you see as his problems and give him a thorough assessment and massage. I am a trained equine shiatsu practitioner and know the huge benefits of this therapy on a horse's mind and body, so do consider finding a therapist in your area. With both massage and shiatsu, you can also learn simple techniques you can use yourself on your horse (see Further Reading and Useful Contacts, page 150).

A logical plan is to ride your horse gently on his stiff side and not avoid the issue, which will do him no good. If he does not become evened up you and he will never be comfortable and will not progress.

- *Start by asking for a little flexion and bend that way on straight lines, around very shallow corners and wide, sweeping curved tracks – nothing less than a 20m circle to start with.*
- *Shallow loops with flexion to his stiff side are also good, as are two-loop serpentines in a 20m by 40m school and three-loop ones in a 20m by 60m school (see page 45).*
- *Don't expect him to do a full circle at first if he finds it hard, and don't keep up a sustained flexion to his stiff side.*
- *Increase this work gradually, as he won't loosen up overnight and making him very uncomfortable will not create good associations.*
- *As soon as you get a good result, cease your aids and praise him, then ask him to hold it a little longer next time, provided he can do this without resistance.*

You will find it a lot easier to straighten your horse if he is used to at least basic lateral work. Leg yield to straight to leg yield is a good exercise, as his straightness will improve when you come out of the leg yield (see pages 52–53). Shoulder-in, particularly to his stiff side (to stretch those contracted muscles on his soft side) creates gentle bend and, again, improves straightness (see pages 56–57).

EXERCISE 2 – USING POLES

- Make a corridor on the ground with poles, or use buckets, blocks or cones if you have no poles.
- Walk, trot and canter your horse down it both ways.
- Gradually narrow it so that it is just one horse's width and there is just room to the sides for his feet.
- As you go down this corridor, really loosen your seat and legs and get the feel your horse when he is held straight by the poles.
- Look straight ahead to some landmark or marker.
- Use a variation of this exercise to create curved tracks – probably the buckets, blocks and cones will work better for this than poles.
- Practise bringing your horse's shoulders round every time you reach a joint, together with a forward nudge of your inside seatbone. Place your outside leg back as a preventive to remind him not to swing out his hind feet.
- Set out poles round a corner to help keep your horse on a curved track and discourage him from 'falling in'. The rider can help that problem by slightly weighting the outside seat bone and stirrup and giving on-off squeezes with the inside calf. Keeping the leg on in a steady support can cause many horses to actually lean on the inside leg; horses tend to lean into sustained pressure but move away from intermittent pressure.

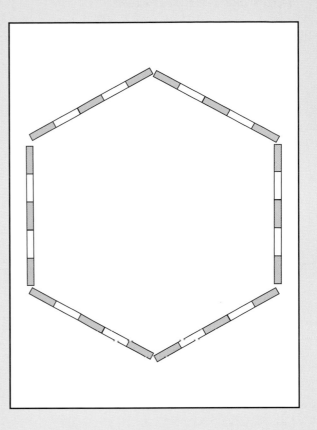

Create large hexagons out of poles on the ground, ideally in corridor format as these guide the horse better.

Using a narrow corridor of poles helps to teach horse and rider straightness in walk …

… trot …

… and canter.

EXERCISE 2 (CONTINUED)

If corners are your or his problem:
- *create tramlines with poles or cones around a corner and take them in walk, trot and canter*
- *be sensible about the faster gaits: asking for too much and going too fast can frighten your horse and put him off – although you may be surprised at what he can do, how much it makes him think and how much he will probably enjoy it.*

Poles can also be used to help with **leg yield** *(see overleaf and pages 52–53):*
- *make a single line of poles, or a corridor of your horse's length from tail to nose so that there is plenty of room for his feet, initially from the quarter line to the track*
- *leg yield* **calmly** *along it*
- *as you do not have the direction to worry about, you can concentrate on your aids for keeping him angled sideways to the track and for rhythmic, sideways movement.*

Lucy and her largely Belgian Warmblood mare, Coral, practise walking through a corridor round a corner.

If your horse becomes crooked, bring his forehand back in front of his hindquarters, as here, rather than the other way round. To do this he has to lighten his forehand by taking his weight back a little, which is what we aim for during most of our schooling.

Lucy and Coral canter fast round a corner through the corridor, bang on line with plenty of energy and engagement from the hindquarters (note the hind leg coming well forward) and in great balance. If Coral had been struggling to maintain her balance, her head would have been turned to the outside of the curve, her quarters would probably have swung out and, at this speed, she may well not have made it round the turn without taking a few blocks with her!

CHECKING YOU HAVE ACQUIRED STRAIGHTNESS

Try to find a school with mirrors and make good use of them, even for only half an hour. Rope in your friend again and ask her for a progress report so that you can see how your work improves. Try to ride your horse regularly on a virgin surface so that you can clearly see the tracks he makes.

And finally – the acid test – get someone to record you and your horse with a camcorder during a schooling session and try and be objective, giving yourself marks out of ten as though you were someone else whom you didn't care a toss about!

Perfect straightness in virtually all circumstances is an advanced state of schooling and, like all of the other scales, you will have to revisit specific straightness work constantly to keep you and your horse up to scratch.

Mirrors are the only real way of checking your straightness and position, if you have no help on the ground.

HOW IT RELATES TO THE OTHER SCALES

To repeat, the scales are interdependent and without reasonable to good Straightness, your work on the other qualities will not have its full effects on your horse's performance. If he is basically crooked, your lateral work could be useless or even harmful, and because it makes him uncomfortable to go crookedly under saddle (even though he may do it when free) he will not be Relaxed although he may manage Rhythm quite well! His Contact will be faulty and he could either avoid it or resist as his discomfort becomes apparent. Impulsion should not be attempted until the horse is reasonably straight, because working with thrust and engagement into a crooked outline can encourage him to develop compensatory movement and the wrong musculature for a balanced riding horse. Because of all this, he will never even approach Collection.

There is little point having your horse schooled by someone else because he is crooked, if you yourself are also crooked. If you get yourself straight and engage some good help from the ground, such as a good bodyworker for your horse, an empathetic and sensitive teacher and a knowledgeable, good friend, you will find that Straightness is not overwhelmingly difficult to achieve.

Impulsion

Impulsion is a strong upward and forward thrust from the horse's hindquarters, which makes you feel as though you are being pushed up in an arc from behind.

WHAT IS IT?

Impulsion is contained, directed energy. It is a combination of power and thrust from the hindquarters and legs, which travels up and through the horse's body, giving his rider what I call 'that power-boat feel', pushing you up and forward from behind. The feeling is such that an unwary rider can be thrown backwards in the saddle, like being pushed back into the seat of a suddenly accelerating sports car. *However,* impulsion in the horse, although it gives you that sort of feel, has nothing to do with speed.

A very common mistake some riders and trainers make (owing to a lack of understanding) when trying to get impulsion is to chase the horse on too fast, usually in trot. This is often done initially to 'get him going forward', whereas, as discussed earlier, speed is not forwardness. When a horse and rider reach the point of needing to master impulsion, speed again is often the result of the rider applying the legs for more energy but being unable to contain it at the front end because she and her horse have not mastered Contact. The horse does not accurately respond to a light contact, so the result is usually a 'held-in' horse with a shortened neck and an exaggerated leg action – an ugly and incorrect picture.

Speed actually makes achieving impulsion impossible. Too fast a speed:

- stiffens up the horse
- puts him on his forehand
- over-stresses his forelegs
- inclines him to lean on the bit, or come behind or 'over' it
- puts him out of balance
- can frighten or worry him, and
- is uncomfortable and unpleasant for both the horse and the rider.

The three main points for you to learn to feel and aim for are:
1. the tempo (speed) and rhythm *do not* increase
2. you feel an unmistakable surge-and-lift from behind
3. the horse lightens up in hand.

Good impulsion as shown by the engagement of the hindquarters and active use of the hind legs.

ASSESSING AND IMPROVING IMPULSION

1

In some early attempts at impulsion, five-year-old Clancy is holding back despite Sally's tactful contact; his back is down and he is not tracking up.

2

Many good-looking horses with naturally free paces get away with going like this which, to an unknowledgeable eye, looks good – cruising along but not actually 'in gear'. Clancy, who is rather tense by nature, is a little behind the bit, despite Sally's very light rein, and is not putting in much effort.

3

This is better. He is calmly accepting a light contact and is starting to use himself and think about engaging his hind end.

4

After a few minutes work, Clancy really lights up. He is concentrating and thrusting forward from his hindquarters in an early effort at real impulsion. His hindquarters are engaged, his hind legs stepping well under his body and pushing. He is using his shoulders well, not going mainly from his elbows, as he begins to turn in off the track. Sally's handling of this highly strung horse is a model of old-school equestrian tact and the advantages of allowing a horse to find his balance under a rider from the start of training, as opposed to the currently common method of trying to 'fix' the horse in place with a hard, unyielding contact, sometimes used under the guise of 'support'.

The most obvious quality you feel when your horse is in impulsion is the *forward and upward* thrust from his hindquarters behind you: this is unmistakable. If you do not feel this, your horse does not yet have impulsion.

At the same time, the forehand lightens (provided you allow it to with a very light contact). If you have any sensation that your horse is pulling at you, running away with you, taking a strong contact or even 'going downhill', he is 'on the forehand' with his weight and balance too far forward. You'll have a heavy feeling in your hands and might even feel that he is tipping you forward.

If you feel that your horse is not going forward (dealt with in detail earlier) or listening to your leg aids, you definitely do not have impulsion and must go back to establish forwardness before you can go any further.

An impulsive horse is also light in hand and manoeuvrable or controllable to a fairly fine degree. You can easily lengthen and shorten his stride in any gait, which results in, respectively, faster or slower tempo (speed). You increase or decrease speed by altering the length of the stride, *not* by quickening or slowing his natural rhythm. Longer strides equals faster tempo, and vice versa.

When watching a horse, look at his hindquarters and legs and his back. You should be able to see that his hindquarters are dropped, with noticeable muscles working, hind leg joints flexing and opening actively and the hind legs reaching well under his belly and pushing.

In front, his neck should *not* be shortened and squashed in by the rider but extending out, lifting at the withers and shoulders, his poll the highest point of his outline and his face just in front of the vertical. His muzzle must look calm and normal, not twisting about with wrinkled, oval-shaped nostrils and froth splashing everywhere, which indicates discomfort and distress.

Aim for impulsion gradually as the horse strengthens. He needs to be active, supple and forward to achieve it, so ask yourself whether or not you have developed and instilled in him the habit of willingly, energetically and instantly obeying his rider's aids without hesitation – in other words, is he forward?

At this stage in the scales, the horse is a novice but not green. The work he has done so far should have made him fairly fit and strong. He needs to have Relaxation and be calm but alert and with energy in reserve. His Rhythm will be confirmed and he will be content with a light Contact (rider permitting) while also understanding the nuances of its variations.

Before you start on Impulsion, your horse may well have been going along quite nicely, listening to you, going forward and cooperating with your aids in good horizontal balance; that means he is not on the forehand but not particularly taking weight back on to his hindquarters yet. Impulsion, which is on the cusp of Pushing Power and Carrying Capacity (see Preparation, What Are The 'Scales Of Training'? pages 4–5), is your next step, putting the power and verve into his body and mind.

It seems that this horse is going fairly fast but is not lowering his quarters and pushing from behind. The rider has given him a comfortable length of rein and could help him by slowing down, putting her legs back from the hips and then tactfully asking for more energy at the new tempo.

PROBLEMS DUE TO LACK OF IMPULSION

Without mastering the Impulsion scale, your horse will go no further in his training. You may not experience any problems, and your horse can carry on working adequately at his existing level, but there will be no progression to Collection – the top of the tree – because it cannot be attained without your horse first experiencing and benefiting from impulsion.

When jumping, your horse will find it all much harder work without impulsion to help launch his body into the air and to get away on landing with agility and push. It is an awful feeling tackling a course of jumps, or even just one, when you have no feeling of power in the engine.

Older horses, too, can benefit from gymnastic work to help keep, or make, them muscled up, working towards impulsion. Here Thorney is going flat, too fast and shows tension in his head and neck, but …

… some minutes later he is starting to round up and use himself better.

It is extremely common and easy for riders to mistake speed for impulsion, and this is often the result. The horse will not only have shorter strides than when going correctly but he will be unbalanced on to the forehand. This is shown in this photograph by the horse having his right fore still on the ground while its pair, the left hind, is well off the ground: the two should land and lift together in trot.

TECHNIQUES TO HELP FIND IMPULSION

You must be sure that you are well balanced and straight in the saddle, capable of maintaining a loose seat, steady hands (so that they do not fly up in the air as he thrusts forward like a bullet out of a gun – well, maybe not quite at first!) and can use your legs effectively down the whole of their length, making your heels your last resort. In fact, it is better to tap with your whip than kick with your heels.

Try to learn to feel which hind leg is coming forward at which moment as this is when to give your aids if you possibly can.

- Keep your seat and legs completely relaxed with no contraction, stiffness or tension, so that they just move naturally and passively with your horse. He needs a completely loose rein so that he can move naturally, letting you feel, through your seat and legs, how his back is moving.
- When you have been walking around like this for a few minutes, you will feel that his back dips and rises under your seat as he walks along (stiff riders never feel this). As a hind leg lifts and comes forward, that side of his back loses its support and so drops; your relaxed seat will drop on that side with it.

- As the hind foot lands and pushes the horse forward, the back on that side will lift under that side of your seat, pushing it up with it.
- The ribcage also swings from side to side during this process like a barrel on a rope. So, as the left hind lifts and comes forward and the left side of the back drops, the ribcage and belly swing to the right, moving your right leg outwards, and vice versa. This 'makes room' for the hind leg to come forward without any possible obstruction from the belly.

The ideal moment to time your leg aid is when a hind leg is in the air, because that is the only time the horse can move it to respond to your request. When the foot is on the ground, it is weight-bearing and pushing, so cannot answer your aid.

Be sure that you can keep your hands independent of your body (see Chapter 3, Contact) as there is nothing more likely to put off a horse from going freely forward and creating impulsion than the expectation and fear of a sock in the mouth (a very uncomfortable or even painful stop signal) as he responds to your aid for it.

Really relaxing your seat and legs (ideally without stirrups) is an ideal way of learning to feel the movements of your horse's back and legs.

Learn to ride with one hand so that, if necessary, you can put your reins in one hand and use your schooling whip to 'tap him up' without fear of giving him an unintentional signal in his mouth. This is easier to do if you are riding in a single-rein bridle as you just put the rein between your index and middle fingers. In a two-rein bridle, it depends on how you choose to position the reins in each hand. Most people ride with double reins in one hand with the two bridoon reins outermost and the two curb reins innermost, all separate. The changeover and back again needs practice!

When something goes wrong in schooling it can often be traced back to a previous stage not having been adequately absorbed, or to the schooling and progression having been rushed – a very common mistake. If this occurs, step back down the ladder to find out where the problem originates and give that rung, or scale, more attention.

EXERCISES

Perform work in the manege, or out hacking, that brings the horse's weight on to his hindquarters, such as shoulder fore, shoulder-in and shoulder-out (see pages 56–60). Don't do this to excess, obviously. Also use transitions, half-halts and pole work.

EXERCISE 1 – ASKING FOR IMPULSION

- *Ride trot shoulder-in into a corner leading to a short side.*
- *Shoulder-in along the short side if he can go this far (he should be able to do this at this stage).*
- *Turn the next corner and straighten up on the diagonal to change the rein.*
- *As you straighten, ask for impulsion. Your trip along the diagonal should produce significant impulsion as he straightens into it.*
- *Remember to be happy with just a promise of it and a couple of strides as your horse learns about it and becomes stronger.*
- *If you can only get a few steps of shoulder-in, fair enough, but then turn off the short side maintaining your bend and flexion.*
- *Then straighten the horse and take him down the school, either on an 'unofficial' diagonal or a straight line.*

Make it a policy to ride into your corners with energy and thrust, because many horses slow down, even fractionally, as they turn. Use shallow turns at first as deeper turns can constitute part of a circle as small as 5m, which is asking a lot of most horses and will over-face them. If you can easily maintain the energy round the corner you should get good impulsion as you come out of it on to the straight provided you give your aid quickly enough. Take advantage of his relief at working straight again!

Circles, lengthening and shortening of stride and transitions (see page 61) also develop thrust and impulsion provided the horse is balanced and straight, otherwise they feel most uncomfortable to him, and you, and do more harm than good. Correct halts (see page 36), rein back (see page 63) and walk to canter (see below) develop the hindquarters and legs and the horse's balance.

EXERCISE 2 – WALK TO CANTER

Many horses like performing walk to canter and find it natural (they often do it in the field).

- *Walk around a corner making a part-10m circle.*
- *Feel, with your seat, which hind leg is coming forward through the air (that side of his back will dip and, if your seat is correctly loose, it will dip with it).*

- *Warn him that you are going to ask for canter by putting your inside seat bone and shoulder slightly forward, release your inside rein contact a little and try to give your normal canter aid as his outside hind is in the air. Remember, he cannot use his leg to start canter while it is on the ground.*
- *If you cannot feel this moment, watch his inside shoulder and give the aid as his inside forefoot lands because his outside hind will be coming forward at that time.*

EXERCISE 3 – IMPROVING IMPULSION

Here is a useful sequence of movements to achieve and improve impulsion:

- *ride on a large circle and do shoulder fore or shoulder-in (see pages 56–58) on the circle*
- *straighten him on to a straight line and immediately ask for medium trot*
- *then change rein and go back to your circle on the other rein and repeat this sequence.*

The circle makes your horse push particularly with his inside hind (the shoulder-in enhances that) and his outside hind must travel and reach more. Going on to a straight line is a mild relief for the horse as it is easier work, and he is happy to go forward, anyway, but particularly into the freedom and movement of medium trot. This exercise develops both the muscular effort and the forward energy needed for impulsion.

Working up and down *gentle* slopes is very good strengthening and balancing work to prepare for impulsion. The horse should be encouraged to engage his hindquarters and hind legs and lift his back, and work lightly up to the bridle without being 'held in' or restricted. Long and low work on gentle slopes for more novice horses is also good development work.

STRENGTHENING WORK

Because impulsion requires more effort from the hindquarters, you must develop their strength and suppleness before gradually asking your horse to start giving it to you. If you simply ask him for more energy before he's stronger, he will probably just try to go faster, not really understanding what you want.

This is the kind of work needed to strengthen his hindquarters and legs:

- work uphill, initially gentle slopes in walk on a loose rein so he can get his head down and push, with you leaning slightly forward in a light seat to lighten his quarters and help him
- progress slowly until he can canter easily up a moderate hill in a working outline, on a light contact in self-balance. He needs to be reaching his neck forward and down, flexing at the poll slightly but always with his face in front of the vertical, and at the jaw joint just below his ear (necessitating a loose enough noseband) so that he can accept and gently play with his bit. Holding him in and up will result in incorrect use of muscles, not least those of the back, and in a horse unhappy in his mouth
- work in water. If you can find some with a safe bottom and that comes almost to knee height, this will be enough to make him work harder and push from behind. If the water is too deep he will struggle, strain himself and develop the wrong muscles. Again, he needs to get his head and neck down, working into a light but present contact. A few minutes of this is enough to start with, progressing to about ten minutes, which is pretty hard work.

The advantages of working uphill and in water are tremendous, as they muscle up the whole horse, not only the hindquarters, and are good cardio-vascular exercise. Like any fitness work, you must progress slowly:

- work over poles. This very often perks up horses and makes them lift and use themselves
- at first use single poles on the ground, gradually building up to a line of six. Use walk initially, then progress to trot and on to canter as he strengthens
- to intensify the work, raise the poles on brick-sized wooden or plastic blocks, ultimately to a height of about 15cm or 6in. Set the poles at a comfortable distance for him in each gait
- perform transitions (see page 61) and lengthen and shorten strides within all gaits and from gait to gait, being sure to maintain his natural rhythm.

Clancy is tackling a line of trotting poles keenly but is going a little too fast, rather than pushing from behind, as evidenced by his right fore – which is slower to leave the ground than its partner in trot, his left hind. Therefore, he is just a little on the forehand. To go with impulsion he needs to use his hindquarters more, in a rounded outline.

Having kicked the poles a couple of times, he is keen to lift his feet but at the expense of raising his back and pushing from behind.

This is improving, with more push from the hindquarters. He needs to stretch his head and neck down and out a little more, then his back will lift and his hindquarters will be able to come under and engage more easily.

RIDING FOR IMPULSION

With a horse who has come through the scales to this point and is going as described overleaf, you simply need to ride him forward with a little more energy into your normal contact. However, bear in mind the comments about speed and be very alert and sensitive to any attempt by him to speed up instead of thrusting more; be prepared to use tactful half-halts if he does (see page 62) and to cease your aids and praise him the moment you feel that unmistakable surge from the hind end that is impulsion.

Also, you will feel the forehand lighten and 'rise' a little if you have done it properly and he has responded correctly. Do not be tempted, then, to increase your contact: keep it light and with your horse's nose just in front of the vertical and allow him to stretch his neck forward. At this stage, he should be working with his eyes about level with his withers (ask your observer to help again) and be lifting his neck up from the base and reaching it forward – and you must let him for correct, comfortable, even exhilarating movement.

Use of the whip

With some horses, a carefully placed tap with the whip can be useful to create more energy and help direct him. Placed here, the whip can help straighten a horse by moving the forehand (in this case to the left) and, during extended work, can encourage more activity from the shoulder and foreleg.

A touch or tap immediately behind the leg emphasizes the leg aid and promotes lightness as it can prevent the leg aid becoming strong or degenerating into a kick.

Used further behind the leg, the whip helps to move over the hindquarters and stimulates hind leg activity.

Used well back on the thigh, it acts as a clear prompt to a horse to move his hindquarters over or to produce more energy and effort from the hind leg.

EXERCISE 4 – RIDE FOR IMPULSION

Your horse will find working on straight lines easier than circles, so use these at first.

- *Take up sitting trot, stay very soft and light in your seat and incline your body a fraction forward from the hips, so as to lighten his quarters and allow him to lift his back.*
- *Take your legs back a little from the hips to their behind-the-girth position to activate his hind legs, and give alternate on-off squeezes with them in time with his normal rhythm.*
- *Use your left leg as his left hind comes forward to stimulate it, and vice versa. Remember, you cannot stimulate a leg to action when it is rooted on the ground.*
- *Sit still and balanced when you do this and be sensitive to any tendency in him to rock from side to side because of your alternate leg aids. If he does, lessen the pressure of your leg aids and use only two or three taps or squeezes with each leg.*
- *Stop the aids and assess what he gave you in response.*

Your horse will find that the only thing he can do is step forward more with his hind legs, tucking under his pelvis a little, but, understanding your contact, he will not try to surge forward faster. The result, almost certainly, will be a more supercharged feel, more power, more life, a lifted back – and maybe a buck and a squeal at the pleasure of this new sensation!

Be thrilled with just a few strides of this at first, remembering to stop your aids and say a very enthusiastic 'Good boy!' as soon as he gives it to you.

POINTS TO WATCH FOR

You most certainly do not want the horse going 'over the bit', overbending, coming behind the bit and shortening and squashing in his neck or, conversely, taking up a firm contact, leaning on the bit or actually pulling, going on the forehand or boring into the ground. Another possible fault is that the horse might start to go crookedly if he is having problems of strength or contact. These are all caused by over-anxiety to 'achieve', by insensitive and tactless riding and lack of judgment – in other words, rider error. If a horse does any of these things, it could be that his rider, whoever it is, is pushing him too hard, asking him too soon, or that he is not yet strong and balanced enough for this work.

Return to strengthening work and work on the four earlier scales of Relaxation, Rhythm, Contact and Straightness. Don't hassle him and do not persist with the common attitude of 'riding him through his resistance'. This will only make things worse, ruin the quality of his work and cause him anxiety and discomfort. It is better by far to get correct work a little at a time, and later rather than too early. Be patient.

If he seems reluctant to give you more energy, check that your contact is not too heavy and therefore restraining him. Then use your schooling whip, held right at the end so that you have the use of its full length, to just tap his flank to stimulate his hindquarters. Practise riding with one hand so that you can take the other off the rein and tap with the whip as far back as his hind leg or croup. This is likely to have more effect if you do not do it very often. The surprise element will usually do the job. The one-handed method is useful to know because if you use your whip while holding the rein, you cannot help but give an inadvertent signal in his mouth, which can confuse him.

Do not start asking for impulsion when your horse is getting a little tired. Warm him up and work him in correctly, and work on impulsion when he is limbered up and still enthusiastic and energetic.

If popping over small obstacles helps to spark up his interest, do it. You can use the occasional single obstacle or make jumping grids of whatever length he can do easily. This does not mean that you can never tax him, of course, but do it very gradually or you can ruin his confidence. Grids can be bounce grids (with no jumping strides) or have one,

two or three strides between them. Don't overdo this work: just use it when you need more mental 'go' and, again, don't do it to perk him up if he has been working for some time and is tired.

Working towards the gate, or towards other horses, often produces more energy in some horses, so do use his instinct and natural desires in this way.

If your horse seems reluctant to give you more energy, check that your contact is not too heavy and therefore restraining him.

Using a small jump can spark up a horse's interest in his flatwork and produce more energy. This rider is sitting in a secure, balanced position which, with her hands following his mouth, also gives the horse great freedom over his fence so as not to inhibit and discourage him.

CHECKING THAT YOU HAVE ACQUIRED IMPULSION

Go to your schooling area and warm-up correctly, initially, of course, on a free rein to let the horse loosen up and get the blood, lymph and energy flowing. As he becomes settled, loose and relaxed, take up a light contact and work him in, concentrating on Relaxation, Rhythm, Contact and Straightness.

When he is flowing along in a good outline (nose just in front of the vertical) in rising, working trot with his back and belly up (this should be normal for him at this stage), pick your spot and ask with your legs for more engagement of his hindquarters and a few strides of impulsion, while lightly restraining him from speeding up with your normal, light contact. Keep your rhythm constant to guide him, and you should feel that power and upward surge from his hind end as soon as you tap or squeeze with your legs.

If your preparation has been correct, he should give you at least a feel of lift and more energy and perhaps a couple of strides or so of moderate impulsion the first time you ask.

If he does, you are well on the way. If not, revert to your earlier scales and to your strengthening work with him, and try again in a week or so.

- Be tactful and confident, neither weak nor 'grinding'.
- Use exercises that your horse can do confidently.
- When you simply ask for forwardness, does he give it to you at once?
- When you ask for impulsion, does he feel as though he wants to give it to you but lacks confidence, or does he just speed up? (The probable causes, in these cases, will be, respectively, too firm or too wishy-washy a contact.)
- If, on the other hand, you prepare properly, mentally rehearse what you are going to do and how you are going to ask him, on your first attempt you ought to get a good effort. Then you will know you are on the right track and, with time, tact and patience, it will come.

HOW IT RELATES TO THE OTHER SCALES

Although you can ride happily without ever reaching Impulsion, it is the icing on the cake and, as mentioned, you will never achieve Collection without it. It is *so* exhilarating and puts the quality, verve and excitement into everything else you do. All your work from the other scales gets that finishing touch, a polish, when done with impulsion and, from your viewpoint, it is thrilling to ride. Although not all horses can achieve Collection, all well-prepared and well-ridden horses, and ponies, can achieve Impulsion. Horses love the feeling and it is one of those major advantages to being a working horse – if they are well-educated and treated, some horses start to use what you have taught them on their own initiative and offer impulsion voluntarily during work – this really is heart-warming.

A good, impulsive trot with the horse working in excellent posture and clearly tracking-up.

Collection

Now you are approaching the top of the training ladder. Not all horses can achieve Collection but it's useful to try provided you do not persist in asking for something your horse clearly cannot give. If he has achieved good Impulsion, in balance and without excessive speed, this is much more than most horses manage

WHAT IS IT?

It is a state in which the horse can produce lift in the forehand by taking his weight back on to lowered hindquarters. He is in perfect balance and self-control (known as self-carriage), with strong hindquarters producing forward energy and carrying the weight of the horse and his rider. The horse has to be able to work on the lightest of contacts and the rider must aim for this: the traditional standard for full, true collection is that the horse can work 'in self-carriage on the weight of the rein'. This achievement is the proof that all the previous schooling has been correct and that his rider/trainer has the right attitude to horsemanship. The horse's weight being borne further back

lightens the forehand and the contact, and causes the head and neck to be carried higher but still pushed up from the base and arched out. All of this frees the shoulders of some weight, saving the horse's forelegs and giving the rider an exhilarating feeling of featherlight control – to the extent that, on a horse with whom she 'gels', she feels that she has only to think her aids to the horse and he will comply.

Heavy or even firm contact, strong leg aids and spurring, and constraint and restriction of the head and neck, with the front of the face behind the vertical, have no place in true collection; neither have exaggerated, unnatural movements of the horse's legs nor a rider who is moving very noticeably in order to achieve collected movements. If any of these are seen, the horse is not in true collection.

Canter pirouette is one of the most advanced movements asked for in dressage tests. This horse and rider are performing it without difficulty and it is good to see the rider looking up and where she wants to go instead of down at her horse, which is so common and appears to oppress horses.

Collection is used, and necessary, for the more advanced airs or movements such as flying changes, half-pass, full-pass, passage, piaffe and canter pirouette, not to mention such High School movements as the airs above the ground, performed by the world's few top classical academies and such life-saving movements in war and bullfighting as canter to the rear, canter full pass and canter on three legs (necessary to get away if your enemy has cut off one of your horse's legs).

An excellent trot half-pass, showing good crossing, energy and not too much flexion and bend, which are common faults.

Collection is the culmination of all the scales that have gone before and is the end purpose of all riding schooling. Unfortunately, many horses never attain it because, a suitable rider and trainer aside, they do not have the individual qualities of constitution, conformation, potential strength in the hind legs and hindquarters, the natural balance enhanced by training or the mental tolerance for regular demanding, gymnastic work.

This final scale and stage of a horse's training ideally sees a horse and rider thinking as one, understanding each other perfectly, each helping and guiding the other, absorbed in their movements together and focused. The horse must cruise along in rear-wheel drive in excellent balance and control. Collection makes a horse a better ride, more agile, athletic and manoeuvrable, stronger, easily controllable, with quick responses, and more powerful.

It certainly takes time to build up the horse's muscles so that he physically is able to take his and his rider's weight further back on to his hindquarters. It is not simply a case of 'you've got it or you haven't'. The different degrees of it are built up, like any schooling and fitness programme, until the horse, in High School work, can produce the ultimate in collection: this is levade, in which he 'sits' on very flexed hind legs with his forehand off the ground and his back at an angle of about 45 degrees. Of course, very few people ever experience this, or want or need to, but it is an example of the strength and control that can be achieved with elite High School horses.

On a more practical level, Collection is the full attainment of the Carrying Capacity stage of the scales, which starts with Impulsion – a correct weight-carrying posture, light in hand with pushing power. The stride shortens but increases in activity and energy. However, the analogy often given, of the horse feeling like a coiled spring, is not really accurate because we do not want substantial pressure, or any actual pressure, in the hand end of the spring.

For a horse to acquire the strength to go in collection in full control of his own body, carrying a decent rider, in correct, arched and rounded posture, weight back and going on the weight of the rein, does take a few years to achieve. If a horse is correctly started in work at three years of age, with consistent, patient schooling, he should be a 'made', well-schooled horse (capable of work in collection) by the age of six or seven, depending on his breed and constitution and, therefore, on the rate at which he matures. He can be taken further to develop his individual talents after this. Those who try to save some of those years of schooling by making the horse *look* as though he is in collection do fool a lot of people. Here is how to tell the difference, from the ground and in the saddle.

She's a natural

Although horses and ponies can be seen in natural collection when playing in the field, not many adopt levade of their own accord. However a Fell Pony that I rode and schooled for years used to do this as an objection if we were trying some work with her that she was finding difficult. With her owner, but never with me, thank goodness, she also used to do natural caprioles when very excited – leaping up in the air, kicking out with her hind legs and landing on all fours, although she then used to try to gallop off, which is not part of the High School repertoire! Fell Ponies have a good deal of Friesian blood in them, and Friesians are one of the old Baroque breeds still schooled today in High School airs, so it was not surprising that my Fell friend found it quite natural and easy to use them to express her feelings.

Small canter circles demand a good level of balance and collection. This horse is managing this small circle well.

ASSESSING AND IMPROVING COLLECTION

Remember what has been said about the strong posture required of a riding horse:

- his back and belly should be *up*
- his neck should be pushed *forward* from its base and carried either
  - low and out (in a young or green horse or one being rehabilitated or made fit) or
  - arched up and forward from its base in a more advanced horse
- the highest point of his outline should be his poll
- the front line of his face seen from the side should be just *in front* of a vertical line dropped from his forehead to the ground
- his hindquarters should be flexed more or less (depending on his stage of schooling) at the croup (the lumbo-sacral joint), to tilt the bottom of his pelvis forwards, engaging his hindquarters and bringing his hind legs well underneath his belly. In collection, the horse's hind leg joints are also flexed more, and strong enough for the horse to be able to 'sit' on his back end.
- the demeanour and 'aura' of the horse should be one of controlled ease, strength, balance, majesty and lightness, with a calm face, a soft eye, no excessive froth around the mouth, which can indicate distress, no excessive sweating, no exaggerated actions of the legs and no contortions of the muzzle
- his back and the dock of his tail should swing easily and rhythmically in time with his steps
- his head should appear to be comfortable and steady but not rigidly still.
- there should be no appearance of uncomfortable constraint from the rider, as it is not necessary or correct in true collection.

A horse and rider in good collection. You can see the engagement of the hindquarters and legs and the raised back. Personally I would like to see the horse's face just in front of the vertical.

From this walk – in balance and a generous length of rein allowing the horse to move comfortably – the rider has a good base to bring the weight back, shorten the stride and lift into collection.

FALSE COLLECTION AND LIGHTNESS

If any of these features are missing the horse is not in true collection. Signs of lack of real collection are:
- the back and belly sagging
- the hind legs trailing
- the neck kinking down or wrinkled in front of the withers and appearing short in proportion to the rest of his body
- an anxious, tense look on the horse's face with wide and worried or dull, shut-down eyes, a very mobile muzzle with drawn-back, wrinkled nostrils and excessive froth

- exaggerated limb actions, mistakenly called 'extravagant', and
- no loose swinging of the back and dock but a stiff torso, neck and head with the horse moving mainly from stifle and elbow rather than hip and shoulder.

If the rider appears to be holding the horse firmly by the reins and the horse looks as though he lacks freedom to work, this is a real give-away of lack of collection and that the horse is being held in an outline to give the impression of collection. True collection demands the lightest of contacts – this is a major point of it – preferably just the weight of the rein. It also demands a relaxed, supple, swinging horse whose *natural* action and conformation has been enhanced by his work and whose body finds it little effort to carry a rider.

False lightness is the term given to horses who have developed the habit of going 'behind the bit' or 'behind the contact', not accepting even a light contact and using an over-bent posture to avoid it – backing off, in fact, even though they may be moving forward quite energetically. Such horses may feel light and forward but they are neither.

Of course, as has already been discussed, speed is not in itself a good thing and is a sign that the horse's gaits have not been developed properly. Horses often rush when they are afraid of their work, whereas others become dull and mechanical, with yet others appearing 'lazy' and not wanting to work: this is usually because it is uncomfortable to do so or they do not really understand what is expected of them (both rider/trainer errors). Again, false lightness is not a part of true collection.

Horse gobbledigook

The world of riding is full of jargon, which is meaningless to outsiders and also sounds pretty ludicrous to those insiders who prefer to KISS (Keep It Simple, Stupid). However, perhaps the more insecure feel that being up to speed with the speak tells others that they know what they're on. Here are some of my more commonly used pet aversions:

On the bit: this gives the impression that the horse is pressing down on the bit, which sounds pretty uncomfortable and is exactly what we don't want in light riding. Neither should we actually want a horse to even *seek the contact* now but to accept and work in confidence with a light contact presented by the rider. If you really want to know, *on the bit* means that the horse accepts a light but definite feel on the reins with a relaxed jaw (so loosen that noseband!) and no resistance. The poll is the highest point of his head and neck carriage, which is stretched forward and arched, depending on his level of schooling, and his nose is *in front* of the vertical.

In an outline: are we doing shorthand here? Not at all. 'Outline' means the shape or 'frame' the horse's body is in when he is working. Again, it depends on his level of schooling, but he needs to present a more or less rounded profile, have his back and belly held upwards, his hindquarters and legs tilted under his body and forward, with flexed joints, and his neck pushed out and maybe arched up. His nose must, as ever, be in front of the vertical.

Coming through: through what? Where? This gives no indication at all of what is really meant by this silly little phrase. What it means is that the rider's aids are passing freely through the horse's body due to Relaxation and lack of tension, plus the mastery of a fair degree of Straightness. To be fair to the horse, it should also be taken to mean that the signals the horse is sending to his rider are also passing to him or her without obstruction resulting from crookedness and tension.

On the aids: not quite as bad as *on the bit*, this expression means that the horse is fully attuned and habitually responsive to the rider's aids, with which he complies with Relaxation, Rhythm, forwardness and confidence, in full harmony with his rider.

Working over his back: this is probably my worst favourite. How can any horse work over his own back? It's crazy. *Working over his back* is a close cousin of *coming through*. The horse's back is up and freely swinging, along with his dock, with utter Relaxation in time with his gait. This indicates a horse schooled without coercion and with a correct, horse-friendly and comfortable use of the bit by the rider. Stiffness problems, which are seen at all levels of equestrian endeavour, almost always start in the mouth, head and neck.

Not going forward: I've actually found one that is even worse than *working over his back*. This is often said by inexperienced instructors to even less experienced pupils who are left completely flummoxed by it. They naturally think 'Well, he's not going backwards, what on earth does she mean?' You and I know exactly what it means, don't we? – that the horse is moving with instant, enthusiastic and energetic responses to his rider's aids, in any direction indicated other than up or down. Forwardness is a state of mind, a readiness to do at once, even eagerly, whatever the rider asks.

YOUR HORSE

Does your horse feel as though he is concentrating his energy in his hindquarters, so you are more aware of them than his forehand and mouth? Do you get a forward and up feeling from him? Does he feel as though he is in supreme, unshakable balance on his hindquarters and do you have the lightest contact with his mouth, which is confidently feeling the bit, so that a mere vibration of the rein produces an immediate result? If so, he is in good, true collection.

On the other hand, do you sense tension and reluctance or resistance on his part when you ask him to come into collection? Does it feel as though he is having difficulties? Is he fussing with his mouth and being erratic in his movements? Is he behind the contact and/or overbent yet you are exerting virtually no pressure on the bit? Do you sense that he is not really with you or that you do not have much control? In this case, he is certainly not in collection even though he may appear so to an unknowledgeable observer.

The extension shown by this Iberian horse and his well-balanced rider is excellent, as is his body attitude and the posture of his head and neck – no squashed-in neck or nose behind the vertical and with an obviously comfortable mouth. Because Iberian breeds (Lusitano, Pura Reza Espanol/ Andalusian and Alter Real) are not common, but increasing, in competitive dressage, their conformation and way of going are often misunderstood by judges and commentators in the sport. They are High School horses par excellence yet suitable for riders at all levels because of their normally equable temperaments.

YOURSELF

For yourself, you must be able to sit in excellent balance and a correct position on your horse or you will disturb *his* balance. You need to have an independent seat and hands to enable this and need to be very well past the stage where you even think of manoeuvring your horse mainly with your hands. Your hands should be receiving and sensitively controlling and distributing the energy that is coming through your horse from his hindquarters, generated by your legs and seat bones. Ask yourself if all this is happening and, if not, work on it to improve your ability to work with him when he is in collection because, by this stage, all the above should be second nature to you.

You can improve collection by giving him more time to strengthen up, by sitting still, in a good position and giving him a confident feel by riding him from your seat, thinking with your seat and thighs and using your legs to energize and stimulate him. Remember the 'ride from back to front' idea discussed earlier. Nag yourself about the contact you are making. He does not want *no* contact as he needs to feel that you are there with him, but he must not feel that you are going to pull him around with the bit. He needs to feel that you will direct the energy he produces (at the request of your legs and seat) with light messages via the bit, the reins on his neck and maybe touches from your hands around his withers, so that he knows what you want. A horse in good collection is positively waiting for you to call the tune without creating any discordant harmonies.

Working correctly on a curved track demands balance, correct bend and flexion and good self-control. It is a good exercise for developing and testing collection if done carefully. The rider can help by being aware that many horses lean in on circles or curved tracks they find difficult. To counter this, if it occurs, slightly weight the outside seat bone and stirrup and ask the horse, with the inside leg down behind the girth, to adjust his balance. If that does not help, spiral the horse out on to a larger circle and try again a few sessions later. This rider is looking ahead around the curve of the track, which always helps.

PROBLEMS ARISING DUE TO LACK OF COLLECTION

For many horses, none do arise, but all can benefit from trying to attain collection. If you wish to ride at a higher-than-average level and become a horseman or horsewoman rather than just a rider, you will come to realize, if you do not have collection, that something is missing. The strength, agility and calm, keen responsiveness of true collection is essential for good performance of more advanced movements. If a rider tries to produce them without it, they become a travesty of what they could and should be. Lack of strength and balance make good results impossible and lead to the rider pulling on the reins, exerting a harsh, rigid hold on the horse's head, and gripping with the legs – very far from the light, uplifting type of riding that we should be aiming for at this stage.

TECHNIQUES TO HELP FIND COLLECTION

You need to learn to be able to play your horse like a fish on a line or a car held on the clutch on a hill. Fine nuances of aids from your seat and legs and your hands can give this effect. You need to be able to let go and give your horse the initiative of arranging his own balance at your behest while still being there to direct operations.

By now, your seat and legs should be reliably loose and your legs capable of being held in tone to control them and to use them without stiffness. Your hands must have a life independent of your body, and your upper body, by means of your inner, core muscles, must be mainly erect, held and still, with the movement of the horse being absorbed by the small of your back, your hips and your pelvis. From this point on, and with this body control, you need to attend to developing a close and sensitive feel of the state of your horse's body and mind so that you know when to instruct him, when to give him more freedom to act, and when to leave him to it.

This is something you will develop, if you are open-minded, from your time in the saddle but also your time with your horse on the ground, caring for him and building up a close affinity with him so that you feel confident together and he associates you with security – he knows where he is with you and that place is called Safe.

This photo illustrates well the weight taken on the hindquarters and particularly the hind legs in collection. Look at the extension of the left hind fetlock which is bearing all the weight of horse, rider and tack in canter.

EXERCISES

Most of the exercises and techniques to help you acquire collection are aimed at strengthening the hindquarters and legs and getting the horse's weight back there, to develop the final phase of the scales – Carrying Capacity.

EXERCISE 1 – TRANSITIONS TO A LOWER GAIT, PARTICULARLY CANTER TO WALK

To develop your horse's ability to come into collection, you need to use your sensitivity, described opposite, when performing exercises that will bring his weight back on to his hindquarters and that you have already been using, such as shoulder fore, shoulder-in and shoulder-out (see pages 56–60) on straight lines and circles, transitions within gaits (shortening and lengthening of stride) and from gait to gait (see page 61). Now, you should practise canter to walk, *as this is a very collecting exercise and, in itself, proof of the horse's balance, strength and responsiveness. Try this:*

- *have your horse in an easy canter between working and collected*
- *make sure that your position and body relaxation and tone are impeccable, and your contact light, steady and just in touch*
- *you should both be relaxed and enjoying yourselves with no tension in your minds or bodies*
- *obviously, your inside hip, and your inside shoulder above it, should be slightly forward, maintaining the canter but, ideally, with no need for any other aids*
- *all you need to do at first is bring your inside seat bone and shoulder level with your outside ones to stop the canter. Normally, when you do this your horse will trot naturally as, with your seat out of canter position, it is more comfortable for him to do so*
- *now, though, you do not want any trot strides at all, if possible, so immediately after you have straightened your seat position, take an obvious breath inwards, still your seat and lean your upper body back a fraction, turn both your wrists outwards so that your fingernails face the sky and apply a gentle but unmistakable tension on the reins*
- *read that again and practise it mentally a couple of times. You can also, of course, say 'Walk on' as well, as that will tell your horse for certain which new gait you want.*

This is all done in very quick succession but it works fine if you do it all at once as a complete change of mind and body attitude that your horse will pick up on. The policy nowadays in more progressive circles is to give one aid, cue or signal at a time, but this combination does work like magic when applied as a composite aid.

Your horse is almost guaranteed to come straight down to walk – if only in surprise! This is all done gently but definitely so that he cannot mistake your actions or meaning. It has a clear 'Whoa' effect, which horses seem to understand naturally. If you need an emergency stop for some reason when out hacking, it works a treat when applied a little more firmly. Depending on the circumstances and your presence of mind, if any, you may also want to yell 'WHOA' or, if you are in enviable control of yourself, just command 'Walk on'.

- If you prefer something a little more conventional, go back to the point at which you level up your seat bones and shoulders to discourage the canter.
- The moment you feel your horse coming out of canter, apply a clear but not hard half-halt and your horse is almost sure to walk or give you, if new to the technique, a stride or two of slowing trot.
- A few more tries and he will get the message.
- Once you get your walk, be sure to give him a little squeeze to reassure him to keep walking on.

Sally and Clancy in Relaxation mode.

Variations on a theme

Travers and renvers are often confused but I hope the following explanations will clear things up. They both have similar aims but travers is done earlier in training whereas renvers, being more difficult, comes later.

Travers (quarters-in or head-to-the-wall) is performed as a suppling exercise, to establish compliance with the outside leg, to develop Carrying Capacity (the final stage of the scales system) and to work towards collection and half-pass. However, it can be taught fairly early in the horse's training (before turn on the haunches or walk pirouette) to help with suppleness training. The horse is flexed and bent in the direction of movement with the hindquarters being carried in away from the fence forming a 4-track movement. His body forms a 30-degree angle to the fence (although a novice horse can form less of an angle) and the horse looks in the direction in which he is moving. You can remember which is *travers* and which is *renvers* if you think of T for teeth (to the fence) and T for *travers*, whereas for *renvers* you think R for rump (to the fence) and R for *renvers*.

In both *renvers* and *travers* the horse is 'shaped' in exactly the same way but *renvers* is done with the rump (hindquarters) to the fence whereas travers is done with the teeth (head) to the fence. Horses find *renvers* (quarters-out or tail-to-the-wall) more difficult than *travers* psychologically as they do not seem to derive so much guidance from the fence with their quarters to it as with their heads to it, as in *travers*. Renvers is, therefore, done quite late in the horse's training when you are thinking of collection. It further enhances the horse's self-control, balance and attention to the rider as well as the same strengthening, suppling and carrying effects as *travers*. The horse is bent in and looks towards the direction in which he is travelling, forming a 30-degree angle to the fence.

EXERCISE 2 – TRAVERS

Another useful exercise to build towards collection is the travers (pronounced 'travair'). This exercise is more difficult for your horse than shoulder-in or shoulder-out as, although he is bent and flexed so that he is looking in the direction of movement (see diagrams), he does not have the manege fence to guide his body (this is the job of your outside leg). He moves on, say, the left rein, bent and flexed to the left, with his head out to the fence and his hind feet in off the track.

Travers is a good exercise for suppling and loosening the horse but also for strengthening his hindquarters and legs and adjusting his weight back in preparation for collection. Before attempting it, he needs to be proficient at shoulder-in and -out, and obedient to your seat and leg aids.

When graduating to smaller circles, as a test of and to help develop balance, impulsion and collection, always start by doing them in a corner bordered by a fence. Even if the fence is not close to the horse, as here, the barrier acts as a psychological guide to the horse and makes it easier for him. Rising trot is also easier on him than sitting trot in the early stages.

- *To come into travers with a novice horse, have your horse in a good medium walk on the left rein, say, with good vertical or longitudinal poll flexion.*
- *Ask for lateral poll flexion to the left and place your inside seat bone and shoulder a little forward, with your outside leg back slightly from the hip and giving intermittent squeezes or taps to ask him to bring his hind feet in a little off the track.*
- *Look up and ahead down the track.*
- *This very slight displacement of the hind feet gives him the feel of a new movement and position.*
- *A couple of steps are enough for a first attempt.*
- *Release your aids and let him straighten by straightening up your own position.*
- *Repeat on the right rein.*

On another day:
- *walk a 10m circle in a corner*
- *as your horse's forefeet reach the track on completion of the circle, place your left seat bone and shoulder forward a little and weight the seat bone slightly*
- *look along the track and tap or squeeze with your outside leg behind the girth to direct him, in bend, up the track*
- *use inside open rein to invite him up the track and maintain the left flexion with a light, still contact*
- *your inside leg asks for movement and energy, if he lags*
- *this method does not necessitate his weight coming forward.*

To use travers with a more advanced horse as a forerunner to turns on the haunches/walk pirouette and collection, and encouraging him to take his weight back, ride him on the inside track and take his forehand over towards the fence, flexing and bending in the direction in which you are travelling – i.e. left bend for the left rein and vice versa.

Always try not to apply all your aids at precisely the same moment. With a horse at this level, he should be maintaining his movements without continually being told by you to do so. Simply asking him, then maintaining your position should be enough, but, of course, do intervene if he seems doubtful or comes out of it.

EXERCISE 3 – RENVERS

Renvers and travers are often confused. In renvers (pronounced 'ronvair') the horse goes flexed and bent in the direction of his movement but his tail is to the fence with his forehand in off the track. Horses find this quite difficult and must not be forced into it. Before you tackle it, your horse must be very confident in obeying your aids to position his body, specifically his forehand and hindquarters. He must be working in good self-carriage and able to use his body with suppleness and strength.

Renvers develops the strength of the hind legs as, done correctly the horse works with more weight on his hindquarters while crossing the outside one quite deeply under him (across the inside one) and pushing significantly with both while holding the bend in a light contact. There is no psychological support from the fence to help him so it is an excellent aid to half-pass; it improves collection because of the weight redistribution and the work asked of the hindquarters, and is a good lead-in to extension because of the energy created in the hindquarters.

- To come into renvers, have your horse on the track in a good, impulsive walk on, say, the left rein, flexed comfortably at the poll, and place him at a 30-degree angle to the track as if you were turning off it, by moving his shoulders over. This lightens the quarters a little.
- Slightly weight your right seat bone and ask him for right flexion and bend, your inside leg down immediately behind the girth and your outside leg back from the hip giving intermittent squeezes to ask for lateral movement up the track, where you should look.
- If you need to maintain energy, tap with your inside leg or whip.
- Do not ask for too much angle at first (although eventually some trainers take the angle to 45 degrees) and do not create too much bend in the head and neck: the horse should appear evenly bent around your inside leg.

CHECKING THAT YOU HAVE ACQUIRED COLLECTION

The feel your horse gives you, as described, plus the ease and quick response with which he complies, will confirm that he is in good collection. You should almost get the feeling that you are sitting on a balloon, which is pushing you up and forwards, and that you know your horse will instantly respond to your aids with no lessening of balance and control.

If this is not the case clearly he needs more time and more tactful work. Always check forwardness, straightness and impulsion and go back to work on those qualities and levels in particular if you are having a problem or seem to have reached a plateau in your progress.

Remember that some horses never reach Collection because they do not have the conformation or potential strength, or the physical constitution and mental attitude to absorb it. Most, though, can benefit from a degree of it; you may get just the early stages of a collected 'feel', perhaps, and see how things go from there.

This beautiful mare and her tactful rider are performing a lovely collected canter in self-carriage, with light contact and excellent engagement of the hindquarters.

Degrees of Collection

In addition to the familiar word, collection, there are other expressions connected with it.

Ramener (pronounced 'Ram-un-ay') is a head position in which the horse carries the front of his face very close to the vertical. It is made possible by the vertical/longitudinal flexion of the poll and the first two cervical (neck) vertebrae which are, respectively, the atlas and the axis. The throat must remain open and arched due to the horse's advancing his body towards his head to a comfortable extent rather than the head being pulled in towards his chest, which is common, highly uncomfortable and wrong.

Rassembler (pronounced 'Rass-om-blay') means the highest degree of true collection possible involving the whole body. The horse is completely 'together' and in harmony and balance, truly in contact on the weight of the rein. He is capable of performing such feats of athleticism and balance as cantering on the spot and backwards, doing full pass all the way round the perimeter of a bullring, *passage* full pass, a 360-degree canter pirouette which turns at one hoof's width per stride, and

various other airs at the zenith of a High School horse's accomplishments. *Rassembler* was *de rigueur* in the old, indoor High School displays, which can still be seen in the Baroque classical academies today.

Levade is an extremely collected, High School air demanding great strength, in which the horse raises his forehand from the ground in an approximate 45-degree angle, flexes his knees to draw his forelegs under his chest and takes his entire weight, and that of his rider, if ridden, on deeply flexed hindquarters and legs.

Pesade is a similar air to *levade* but the hind legs are not so flexed and the stance is higher, so it is less demanding of extreme collection than *levade*.

Maybe this horse is not quite ready for significant collection. He has come behind the bit, and his rider has released the rein and is probably asking for forward movement to counteract this. The horse is also flat in the back and his quarters are disengaged with hind legs trailing. More strengthening work will help this tactful rider prepare her horse to try again in a few weeks' time.

EXTENSION

We certainly cannot leave Collection without mentioning what would be the next scale, and with some trainers who use their own individual scales it is, and that is Extension. Unfortunately for many horses, extended gaits, at least in trot and canter, are the most dramatic and the most exhilarating but are often misunderstood.

Correct extensions, especially in trot and canter, are difficult, athletic, advanced movements and are not taught until after the horse is established in performing correct, quality collection because he needs the strength in his hindquarters to power through from behind. The horse also needs very well-established balance because he must be able to extend his strides without falling on to his forehand. Signs of this are heaviness in hand, a downward, boring feeling and tripping up. He must be able to stay balanced, working from the hindquarters, while strictly maintaining his normal, natural rhythm; the faster tempo (speed) of extended gaits is achieved through covering more ground, not by speeding up the steps.

His posture (in extension) should be with his neck stretched out but still rounded and with his nose in front of the vertical while maintaining a light contact.

He also has to work comfortably in a correct posture. It is not only his stride that lengthens but also his whole body and outline. His posture should be with his neck stretched out but still rounded and with his nose in front of the vertical while maintaining a *light* contact. A major mistake is that the rider, or the horse, takes too heavy a contact because the horse is likely to lose, or has lost, his balance. If this happens, he is not ready for this work. This firm contact results in a horse being 'held up' with a shortened neck and an on-the-vertical head carriage, or, in bad cases, a behind-the-vertical head carriage.

During all this, horse and rider must remain relaxed so that the horse is not hampered by tension or excitement, extending calmly and lightly. He must be straight, otherwise not only will the extension be of poor quality but could be injurious to him. As you can see, the work done on strengthening and impulsion not only enables collection but also collection enables extension. As you can also see, this work is far from easy. Extensions are often asked for too soon because riders want to do them, but a lot of problems in future schooling can arise because of this, such as incorrect muscle development, impure gaits, anxiety in the horse, strained backs and forelegs, and mouth problems.

Extended canter au naturel.

So many horses are asked to extend before their collection is established and fall apart by being taken too fast, held firmly 'up and in' (usually showing mouth problems and discomfort), unavoidably flattening their backs, trailing their hind legs and flicking out their forelegs rather than arching them forward from the shoulder. There is no sign of that here. Horse and rider are showing good extension in canter with maintenance of self-balance and posture and with a clearly comfortable mouth. Beautiful!

AIDS FOR EXTENSION

You can encourage your horse to extend by slightly exaggerating the alternate movements of your seat bones, to which he should, by this stage, be responding as a driving aid like your legs; or by sensitively using your legs alternately. The moment to push forward with your seat bones, or to squeeze or tap with your legs, is as each hind foot picks up, to stimulate the hind legs without causing the horse to rock from side to side. So, as always, right seat bone or leg is applied as the right hind picks up and vice versa. Modern thinking on stopping your aids as soon as you get your response still applies here. You should not need to actively keep telling the horse to keep up the movement you have asked for.

Allow lengthening of the horse's outline by giving him more rein. Open your bottom three fingers as described in Contact – this will give him a few inches of rein without your having to move your hands and arms. If you also need to do the latter, keep it minimal whilst giving him as much rein as he needs to extend and to keep a light contact, or simply let the reins slip through your fingers and take them back afterwards. The less you do, the less likely are your own position and balance to be disturbed. To come out of extension, just lessen the passive movements of your seat, then take a momentarily firmer contact on the bit.

Modern thinking on stopping your aids as soon as you get your response applies here. You should not need to actively keep telling the horse to keep up the movement you have asked for.

A very active hind leg action from this lovely horse, extending his canter in good posture – no shortened neck or over-bending.

Extended walk: during preceding work, you will have been lengthening and shortening your horse's stride, doing free walk on a loose rein not only as a rest but as a physical exercise to encourage supple and full use of the body and to develop and check his balance. Extended walk must obviously be longer than medium walk, with the horse's hind feet landing well in front of the fore prints. His neck can be stretched out more or less horizontally depending on his natural conformation and carriage, and the nose in front of the vertical, of course, but not poking. He should be on a light contact sufficient to maintain a rounded outline.

Extended trot: this is where all your work on impulsion and collection will pay off in the difficult extended gaits. The horse must be thrusting forward with as much impulsion as he can produce *without* racing along or becoming excited, speeding up his steps, going crooked, becoming heavy or losing his balance, while lengthening his outline and covering as much ground as possible. He needs to stretch his neck out, although it should be a little higher than in extended walk, and he must maintain his light contact with his nose in front of the vertical.

Extended canter: the same criteria apply as for extended trot. Be careful not to let it deteriorate into a 4-beat, fast canter approaching a three-quarter speed gallop! Maintain your

light contact and only do a very few steps at a time at first, bringing him back to medium canter and slower, as you wish, to confirm compliance. Keep it relaxed and calm and you should have no problem. Try it at first away from the gate of your school, or away from any other horses nearby, although he should, by this stage, not need such precautions.

Now you and your horse have reached the top of the Training Ladder, trying for and maybe achieving Collection. The feeling of a collected horse working with you lightly, strongly, in control of his own body and in self-carriage on the weight of the rein is ecstasy. Remember that it is very hard work for a horse and he really must be allowed years to develop not only the established physical strength of an athlete but the mental capacity to cope with this work and understand all the aids and their shades of meaning. It is a responsibility and challenge for any rider and most certainly cannot be forced. It isn't collection if it is forced. The travesties of collection so often seen in both training and competition do nothing but damage the horse's body and attitude and can only be regarded as abuse. With the right attitude, principles, training and schooling, you and your horse will enjoy a sense of real achievement, as well as loving working together.

'The only thing we're interested in collecting is grass.'

Conclusion

I really hope that this introduction to the traditional Training Scales has been helpful, informative and interesting. They can be applied to any horse and provide a reliable guide and framework to work to. Very often, when something goes wrong in schooling, it is because a previous stage was not fully absorbed or carried out. It is simple to step back down the ladder to find out where the problem originates, and to do more work on earlier scales. If problems persist, it may be necessary to call in veterinary help or that of a professional, empathetic trainer or therapist.

BODY ...

It never occurs to very many riders whose horse is a hobby to them that they may be the cause of a problem simply because they are not fit or supple enough themselves to ride well. Riding very regularly helps, but it is not enough on its own to rise above the average, fairly low, level of physical ability needed to even adopt and hold a good position on a horse. Riding uses specific muscles and applies particular stresses on our bodies in a way that no other sport or activity does. If you are not reasonably fit, and developed in a way appropriate to riding, you are putting yourself in more danger than you need to.

The horse world now has plenty of rider-therapists and trainers able to help with this, and there are several books, videos and DVDs about modalities adapted to riders, such as Pilates, yoga, Tai Chi, sports massage, fitness for riders, meditation, Alexander Technique and Feldkenkrais.

If you know that you are completely unfit, just start by walking a lot more (yes, I know time is an issue, but some things just have to give to make room for others). Walking smartly to raise your heart rate and gently stress your muscles can be just as beneficial as jogging and running, with less impact damage. To improve your cardio-vascular fitness, you need to get a bit hot, sweaty and breathless most days of the week, but not so much that you cannot carry on a conversation while you work.

Nurture what you have, get rid of what drags you down as far as you possibly can or try to improve it in some way.

Take the time to loosen up your head, neck and shoulders to relieve tension and prevent stiffness when you ride.

Stretch and flex your hands and roll your wrists around to help ensure that your contact is sensitive and comfortable.

Specific exercises to loosen you up for riding, properly done with intent, not just for a giggle, are almost essential, particularly as you, shall we say, mature. Stiffness is a major enemy of performance. You need to do the exercises most days, certainly before and after you ride, if you want to maintain a supple, adaptable body. Rolling your head around, circling your shoulders up and back, swinging your legs not only backwards and forwards but out to the sides, circling your ankles and flexing and shaking your hands and wrists may all sound familiar, but do you actually do them on a regular, and therefore productive, basis?

... MIND ...

Busy lives create busy, fatigued minds. Learning to relax for yourself is essential to give your brain a bit of a break, whether you achieve that by something active and fulfilling such as gardening, dancing, taking your dog out, playing with your children or something else in that category, or by means of something such as meditation, listening to music, having relaxing, scented baths or a professional massage now and

again, or whatever else does the trick for you. You don't have to spend very long each day on such things but doing *something* every day will make a surprisingly big difference.

Your mental attitude, not only to your riding but to your life in general, can be a real life-changer. Getting your life's priorities in order and cutting out the chaff – commitments you are often talked into or 'feel' that you 'have' to do – can give you many more hours a week to spend on the things that really matter. Your mind-set can make or break your entire relationship with your horse and your attitude to him, whether or not you compete.

Ask yourself whether your glass is always half full or half empty, and whether you find yourself thinking and speaking negatively. We can always improve our lives, and there is always someone worse off and better off, it seems, than us. The old-fashioned maxim of counting your blessings is a great way to straighten things out in your head.

Do not associate with negative people, but if you have to, answer them back in a positive way that will protect your own way of thinking. Spend as little time with them as possible.

Competition nerves spoil many people's associations with their horses. If, deep down, you realize, on reflection, that you don't really like competing but are 'expected' by others to do it, stop it. If you are mad about it, ask yourself why you feel the need to keep beating other people. It can be even more rewarding and enjoyable to ride for its own sake, to be the best you can possibly be for *your* sake and that of your horse, rather than using someone else's standards in a competitive way to judge yourself. Everyone is different and it is more productive and fulfilling, and also important, to do your own best rather than compare yourself to other people. In any activity, there are basic standards that you need to accomplish, but I find it best to do this, maybe with help, in your own way.

Never run yourself down and say that you are a terrible rider, or that you will 'never be able to do that'. You really don't know what you can do until you try, and if you do try but think you haven't done very well, try again and things will almost certainly improve.

Of course, you have to be reasonable with yourself and not set silly goals. Even setting any goals at all can be counter-productive and stressful to some people, but others need them, not only to make any progress, but also to actually achieve anything. The correct attitude to adopt is the one that works for you.

Only you know how you feel inside, how your body is reacting and how you think about a certain thing.

If you are still not happy with yourself and your life, pretend you are a counsellor and are being paid to counsel yourself. You also really care about this person who has come to you for help. Approach your life from that viewpoint, write things down as though they were about someone else – your relationships, your work, your family, your friends, your horse, your dog, your ambitions or 'would likes' and particularly your 'don't wants', and review everything from a caring outsider's point of view. It can make a big difference and help you to see things as they really are.

Losing confidence in the saddle is very easy for many people. It only takes a few bad falls and a realization that the effects of some old injuries are going to be with you for the rest of your life to put some people off riding for good. The ideal way to get your confidence back, I find, is to find a real plod and just sit on him or her. Then, when you get fed up with that, try walking, maybe being led, then when that gets boring have a trot and so on.

When you progress to other horses, only ride those you trust, bearing in mind what we all know – that there is *always* some element of risk in riding or having to do with horses. Take professional help, if you like, be reasonable with yourself and don't lie to yourself about your prospects of doing what you want. Amend your wants to what you are fairly certain you can reach – one bite at a time – and above all, think Positive.

Canter pirouette is often badly performed, even at the 'highest' levels, but not here. The horse clearly demonstrates the stress placed on his hind end. He is appropriately flexed and bent, not excessively so, and the only improvements would be for his rider to look up and around the pirouette track, and give the horse a touch more freedom on his inside rein.

... AND SPIRIT

The spiritual aspect of horses and riding comes into this largely in the form of your attitude to your horse. It was always drilled into pupils and students years ago that we had to put our horse or pony first. It is one of life's privileges to be able to ride, we were told, and so we have a duty to consider the horse first rather than regarding him as a servant (still a fairly prevalent viewpoint in some quarters) or, even worse, a possession to do with as we want. This is not the case.

People who regard their horses as friends who are dependent on them for everything, from their daily food and water to the way they are trained and ridden, always have more fulfilling relationships with them, I find. If you have a high commitment to your horse's well-being, the willingness to put his welfare first in your dealings with him and the knowledge to do nothing intentionally to distress or harm him, not only will you feel good about yourself but you will find a close and firm partnership developing between you unlike any other area of your life.

'Thank goodness we've reached the end.'

In a book of this nature, I think it appropriate to finish with a word about the competition sphere and the roles of judges and the administrative organizations responsible for running disciplines, setting standards and making rules. They bear the responsibility of promoting good riding and performance, which can only be the result of correct, humane schooling.

Very many people, unfortunately, ride only to compete and win, rather than treating competing as an adjunct to their life with horses. By giving good marks to competitors showing correct techniques and caring principles of schooling and management (clear to the knowledgeable eye from the way the horse appears and goes), and by rejecting their opposites by marking down those riders who clearly do not understand, apply or even care about these things, no matter who they are, judges and those responsible for their training, selection and monitoring will send a clear message to all in equine sport that rushed, forced and unethical schooling techniques and management methods will not result in high marks and success but in low marks, rejection and a degree of shame.

I do hope that this book has helped you understand the concept and uses of the Scales of Training. It has been written for people who may never have heard of the scales or who may have heard of them but were not sure what they were or how to apply them.

A common misconception is that the scales are like standards that you and your horse need to master before promoting yourselves to the next one up. There is this element to them, but the scales are constantly relevant for green and advanced horses alike. All horses' schooling and performance should be revised during one session a week, using all the scales the horse has mastered so far, to check his grasp of them, his work and whether or not he is ready to learn something else or needs to go back a scale to polish it up.

Advanced, experienced horses can develop problems in their schooling and the scales can be used to trace back to where the problem stems from – maybe Rhythm has become erratic, Contact is dubious as the horse is showing some dislike of it, or perhaps Relaxation needs work as the horse may be becoming nervous of new situations or venues, and so on.

The scales are there to help you, guide you and keep you on track, like a reliable programme, which is simple enough to hold in your head when riding. I hope you make good use of them.

The scales are there to help you ... I hope that you make good use of them.

Further reading and useful contacts

FURTHER READING

Fisher, Sarah, *Know Your Horse Inside Out* (David & Charles) 2006

Hannay, Pamela, *Shiatsu Therapy for Horses* (J.A. Allen) 2005

Heuschmann, Dr Gerd, *Tug of War: Classical Versus 'Modern' Dressage* (J.A. Allen) 2007

Loch, Sylvia, *Invisible Riding: The secret of balance for you and your horse* (The Horse's Mouth) 2003

McBane, Susan, *100 Ways to Improve Your Horse's Schooling* (David & Charles) 2007

McBane, Susan, *Revolutionize Your Riding* (David & Charles) 2007

McBane, Susan, *The Horse Owner's Essential Survival Guide* (David & Charles) 2004

McLean, Andrew, *The Truth About Horses* (David & Charles) 2003

McLean, Andrew and Manuela, *Horse Training The McLean Way: The Science Behind The Art* (The Australian Equine Behaviour Centre) 2005

Silverman, Tony, *Studies in Equitation: The complete book on the art of riding horses* (published by the author) 2002 (Available from Tony Silverman, 19 Lake View, Edgware, Middlesex, HA8 7RT, England.)

Wilson, Anne, *Top Training Methods Explored* (David & Charles) 2004

USEFUL CONTACTS

The Australian Equine Behaviour Centre
Clonbinane Road, Broadford
Victoria 3658, Australia
Website: www.aebc.com.au

The Classical Riding Club
Eden Hall, Kelso,
Roxburghshire, TD5 7QS, Scotland
Website: www.classicalriding.co.uk

The Equine Behaviour Forum
Sea View Cottage, 41 New Road
Shoreham-by-Sea, BN43 6RB, England
Website: www.gla.ac.uk/External/EBF/

TTEAM UK (Sarah Fisher)
Tilley Farm, Farmborough
Bath, BA2 0AB, England
Website: www.ttouchteam.co.uk

Tracking-up™: an independent view
(Quarterly equestrian periodical)
Park End House, Robins Folly
Thurleigh, Bedfordshire, MK44 2EQ, England
Email: annewilsonclassicaldressage@hotmail.co.uk
Website: www.tracking-up.com

Horsewise Self-Study Courses™
(*Affordable, quality learning*)
Carmel Cottage, 50 Marsh House Lane
Over Darwen, Lancashire, BB3 3JB.
Email: horses@susanmcbane.com
Website: www.susanmcbane.com

Acknowledgments

I first wish to thank Sally and David Waters for their usual and extensive help and cooperation in their task of providing the photographs for this book, and especially for arranging such a lovely venue in England for the UK shots. The Hobbs' Comberton Stud is set in a beautiful and ancient landscape and Sally Hobbs and her daughter Emma Gill (riding respectively Comberton Clancy and Thorney) were so patient, helpful and competent in acting as our models. Lucy Corbett and Coral also joined our shoot and I very much appreciate their efforts and good-natured help.

Sally and David's USA contacts also went to a great deal of trouble and have added a valuable international flavour to the book. My thanks, therefore, go to Maya Sniadecky with Flirt and Dulcinea and to Melissa with Stanford. For Jacqui Jacobs with Reggie and Sheri Evers-Rock with Maestro, this is the second of my books they have helped with, so there is a special thank you for them.

Finally, I am truly indebted to Eleanor Holme for her most professional and light-handed copy-editing plus her knowledgeable input. The editorial and production teams at David & Charles, as always, have made the whole project possible and my thanks particularly go to Jane Trollope and Emily Rae who work together, and with their authors, so well.

Index

Page numbers in italic indicate an illustration
not contained in the text page range.